YES! YOU ARE GOOD ENOUGH

TRISH TAYLOR

Yes! You Are Good Enough

by

Trish Taylor

www.trishtaylorauthor.com

Book Cover Design
Vanessa Mendozzi

Developmental Editor
Kari C. Barlow
Editing Team
Jennifer Reeves
Jessica Forbes

ISBN: 978-1-7328655-2-5

CONTENTS

PREFACE

Self-help books can be annoying. I write them and they annoy me too. Especially those that promise the earth, that guarantee they can fix your problem in five minutes. If you have been carrying around your imposter syndrome for a lifetime, I can't promise that you will shake it off with a flick of your hair or a snap of your fingers. I can promise that if you are suffering through this awful curse of feeling that you are not worthy, there is a way to feel better. It doesn't happen overnight. I am a practitioner of a range of techniques that work well. They can be life changing. I have helped people work through issues that have dogged them for decades, yet they still sometimes need a top-up or a reminder they are good enough, that they can do it, and that there are actions they can take to deal with the feelings that arise. I have also worked with people who have had to change their life after dramatic changes in circumstances, often reinventing themselves. I know that wherever you have been and however you have judged yourself up to this point, you can change for the better and move forward.

I'm glad that we have a name for this thing now. If I'm

talking in a group and mention the concept of imposter syndrome, it's common for at least half of those present to relate to the idea, to claim it as their own and sometimes for someone to say, "Oh, wow! That's a thing? I thought it was just me." It's not a disease that needs a diagnosis, and everyone's experience will be different. Let's start with a check-in and then you can see if you think this book will be helpful to you. Check this list and see if any of these give you an ah-ha moment. You might not have these feelings all the time, or in every situation, yet you will know as you read down the list below if I am speaking to you.

Trigger Warning: This list has the potential to make you feel uncomfortable while you are working through it.

- You feel judged by other people.
- You worry you come from the wrong area, family, country, religion, era, school.
- That you have the wrong accent.
- You feel people don't like you—even your friends.
- You compare yourself and feel that you don't measure up.
- You worry you got your job by accident.
- You think everyone else is achieving more than you.
- You believe you are the weakest link in your organization.
- You think you have been lucky so far and your luck could run out.
- You spend a lot of time thinking about what you don't know and aren't good at.
- You speak negatively about yourself.
- You don't believe that you deserve to be where you are.
- You don't always like yourself.
- You heard awful things said about you as a child.

- You think you need a lot more help to achieve your goals than others.
- You worry that you have nothing interesting to say in social settings.
- You think your clothes are all wrong.
- You worry you don't know enough about current affairs, movies, music, politics, fine food, art.
- You worry you don't know enough—period.
- You give your services away for free or reduced price because you aren't confident you are worth full price.
- You go away from social interactions worrying that you said or did the wrong thing, that you looked stupid or that you failed.
- You accept low standards from other people because you don't feel you deserve better.
- You feel resentful of others because they take advantage of you.
- You get paid less than you should and don't ask for a raise because you think you aren't worth it.
- You think everyone looks better than you.
- You feel embarrassed if anyone pays you a compliment.
- You don't do small talk as you think no one is interested in what you have to say.
- You think other people are smarter than you.
- You think people are just being polite when they invite you to events.
- You feel you are usually the least smart person in the room.
- You believe anyone can do what you do and that you are nothing special.
- You believe that the only reason you are where you are today is because you are lucky, got a break, got help or studied hard.

- You think it's probably too late to change.

These feelings and concerns are not true, you just built them up inside your head and had no one to tell you otherwise. I bet you haven't told many people, have you? You've kept this story to yourself or told very few people you feel like this. You walk around looking confident on the surface, and you don't tell people that inside you are terrified you will eventually mess up and be exposed as a fraud. Because we hide these feelings, we don't realize how many others are experiencing the same doubts.

In this book:

- Discover why you don't feel good enough.
- How other people are part of the problem and can be ignored.
- Uncover and challenge your own lies about yourself.
- Banish perfectionism and overthinking.
- Fix your mindset.
- A 28-day program to help you move into confidence.

INTRODUCTION

This book is to help you feel more confident, let go of the negativity and live your life on your terms.

You have been telling yourself for so long that you are not good enough. Somewhere deep within you the voice is an echo of a message you heard, a lie, a miscommunication, or a perversion of the truth. You heard it, or maybe you overheard it and absorbed it until you believed it to be true. The accusing voice in your head is not really you—it's an evil twin who lies. Before you can tell that person to be gone, you have to recognize the lies.

I was raised Roman Catholic. Every year we had a May Procession. It was a religious festival, though to us kids it was about putting on a fancy dress and walking through the streets showing off. It was also a popularity contest. If you lose at a popularity contest, you might believe you are not good enough. It was where I had the self-esteem knocked out of me before I could even spell the word. Our procession had a queen and a small group of attendants chosen from my class. I was around seven years old, and my idealistic kid brain had not yet learned that the Catholic world was as unequal as the rest, and I would not get the same opportunity that everyone else had. The girls' names were written on pieces of paper, and the teacher pulled the names out of a hat and announced the lucky winner. *American Idol* had nothing on the anticipation of winning the golden ticket of May Queen attendant. As the excitement rose, I learned there was no point in getting my little heart's hopes up. A classmate took delight in telling me she already knew I had no chance of being chosen. According to her inside knowledge, the teacher had decided that they would not even place my name in the hat. Apparently, I wasn't right for the prized role, and my family couldn't have afforded the required dress anyway. This was my first experience of heartbreaking disappointment, alongside the shame, guilt, and misery of being singled out as being different. For years after that, circumstances regularly reminded me that my family was not good enough.

While I didn't grow up in abject poverty and never went hungry, I remember being different enough to stand out. Being different because of relative poverty was enough for others to notice me and for me to magnify and internalize that difference.

The reasons we develop these tendencies are varied. As you read further, you might uncover or remember situations, comments, or conversations that have contributed to the way you feel about yourself and your confidence. Equally important, you might recognize things you have said and done that have played a part in others having the same feelings. This is forgivable because you are human. As you learn to recognize the power and potential harm in your words, you can be more cautious. Since I have done work on myself and helped others, I have become mindful of conversations I have had in the past. Although our former actions can be cringeworthy now, we must remember that we are growing and changing, and we must be allowed to forgive ourselves and learn from our mistakes and carelessness.

You Are Not Alone

Do you know who else is worried that they are not good enough? Just about everyone. Discounting the narcissists and psychopaths, those not worried are often those who have proved their worth repeatedly. To reach that point, they had to fail many times, yet failure is a method of feedback so we can learn to do things differently next time. If you never try, you will never succeed or fail, and you will never reach a place where you feel comfortable. Even those who are confident have moments of fear, doubt, and terror, asking "What if I screw up?" When you put yourself out into the public arena, you will probably get criticized. People love to bitch and if you dare to rise, there likely will be someone, somewhere who will have something to say about it.

It's often
the smartest
people who worry
about not being
smart enough.

It might surprise you to discover that some of the superstars you see on the big screen, or those entertaining thousands in stadiums, have moments of sheer terror before they go on stage. They also compare themselves to others in their field and worry that they will not live up to the expectations of those who are supporting and depending on them. There is a reason drug, alcohol abuse, mental health issues, and even suicide are prevalent among the gifted. Living up to expectations and constantly having to prove that they deserve to be where they are, can be mentally exhausting and sometimes intolerable. Substance abuse is often used as self-medication rather than a way to have fun.

PART I

1

IT'S ALL ABOUT YOU

No one else can help you feel better or fix the feeling that you don't belong. You might find it helpful to do some deep work on yourself. One option is traditional psychotherapy, talking things out with a licensed therapist. Another choice, which I made years ago, is to explore and train in alternative therapies and techniques. Through that process, I uncovered many ways that I had accepted beliefs about myself that were not true.

Truth is an important part of discovering why you feel the way you do. Disconnecting from the part of you that believes the lies you have been telling yourself is vital. You need to believe that you are good enough and are prepared to do what you need to make that belief come true. I don't mean faking it until you make it. Though you will begin with a leap of faith that you are good enough, little by little we will make this your reality. I am so excited about the journey you are going on.

You are worth it. I know you have spent a lot of time worrying about other people, not taking care of yourself and doing things you don't want to do, but that is all about to change. Are you up for it? When we have uncovered where your beliefs come from, you will find practical solutions in a twenty-eight-point plan, which you can complete in as quickly as a month or more slowly, at your own pace. Even if you start and have to stop, that's OK, because you can start again. You have spent a lot of time believing the fake stories about yourself; it will take some time to reprogram.

Reality Check about Other People's Opinions

Most of us who struggle with imposter syndrome worry a lot about what others think of us. You need not concern yourself with a stranger's negativity. You can spare a moment to feel empathy for the emotional pain that causes their caustic behavior and then move on to create something amazing in your life. How much does it really matter if someone you know is judging you or your choices? Are you going to let it stop you from living your life to its fullest or stop you from fulfilling your potential?

Have you ever had a great idea that you immediately dismissed as too crazy, too expensive, too risky, too impossible? Look around you. We have driverless cars, the ability to talk to people via video for virtually free, and a million other inventions that would have seemed miraculous just a few years ago. The people behind those innovations had these ideas. They were not a different species; they were living, breathing humans like you. Instead of worrying that their ideas might not work, they were busy figuring out how they could. In this chapter, I plan to challenge some of your beliefs and maybe even dismantle them altogether. Let's begin with some of your own untrue stories. Stop for a moment and think about the things you believe you can't do.

- What do you think is beyond you?
- Who do you look at and think, "I could never do that?"
- What are some things you fear you will never do again?
- What have you achieved that you once believed you couldn't?
- What did it feel like at the beginning?
- Did you ever worry that it would never come together?
- How did you feel when it was completed?
- Was it easier or harder than you believed it would be?
- What can you learn from this?
- Think about the people you admire whose achievements and success seem out of your reach.
- Are they superhuman?
- Did they always have these skills, or did they have to learn them?
- What can you learn from these people?

Make a note of any answers or thoughts. They will be useful when working on your plan.

No one starts out being able to do everything or anything. We all have to learn and start somewhere. When we see success, it is the culmination of weeks, months, and even years of work.

Sometimes I meet people who tell me what they can't do and then I learn what they have already achieved, and it astounds me. Those of us worried we aren't talented often underplay our achievements. Look at the record of things you have already done and store it up as evidence.

You need to believe that:

- Your ideas are as good as the next person's.
- You can change your mind.
- You are a free human; you don't have to do what people ask, tell or demand.
- You can say no.
- Doing things because you have always done them that way is no way to live.
- It is never too late to start, or to start again.

Imagine:
You are on your deathbed. What will your biggest regret be?
You just bought the winning lottery ticket or received a massive amount of money in a legacy.
What would you do?
What would you stop doing now and never do again?
Where would you go?
What else would you change?
Of these things, are there any you can do now?
This is the only life that you will live right here and now.

I moved to the United States from England in 2005. When I left, my parents were in reasonable health, although my dad had not been very well for years. I had a hope that one day they would come and visit me here to see the life I live and meet the friends I have. Time passed, and it became clear that it was unlikely to happen. Now my dad has passed, and at the time of this writing, my mum has dementia and requires full-time care. She will never visit me here. What has that to do with confidence? My parents did not get to do everything they could have in their lives. They did not dream big or have aspirations to live a better life. They accepted their lot, lived in the same cold house for decades, worked hard in often unrewarding jobs and looked at others who were doing better as somehow different. They were talented, smart people yet did not believe there was more out there for them. They did not have unhappy lives, yet it could have been better. Yours can be better. And it starts with believing in yourself—right now.

Thinking Bigger

Begin by dreaming. If another human being has done it, there's every chance you can do it too. You get what you focus on. If you are continually thinking of all the things that can go wrong, they will. When I studied history, we learned that people thought the body could not handle the physical pressure of a train journey. There were fears that women traveling by train at high speed would be at risk of their uterus flying out of their bodies. Imagine if everyone had believed that. When I was a kid, we were still tying cans together to make our own pretend telephones, and the ones in houses had long cords attached. Someone somewhere dreamed of a phone that would fit easily into our pockets, follow us everywhere, and eventually take control of our lives.

Reaching your own goals and dreams rarely happens by accident. Instead, it requires intention, focus, and the willingness to be introspective.

Here are a few things to try:

- Decide today to think about what you want.
- Write down your goals and dreams.
- Identify the people in your life who support you. Spend more time with those people.
- Identify the people who pull you down, hold you back or belittle you. Spend less time with those people.

The Accuser

When you wake in the morning and hear that voice, the mean-spirited, doubting, envious, hurtful, or accusatory voice that tells you you're not good enough, you might find it useful to discover where it came from.

The voice that says you can't do something comes from many sources—friends, colleagues, parents, teachers, random strangers. When I work with clients, I use techniques that help to uncover and identify the voices that inform our beliefs. We store them at an unconscious level, deeply embedded, heard possibly decades ago, yet ultimately accepted as fact. Sometimes the source is obvious. For some of us, a cruel comment or innocent word can cause a lifetime of self-esteem issues, lost opportunities, and heartache.

I originally believed that those with imposter syndrome might not have felt valued as children. As I researched, I learned this is not always true. Even those with the best chance of success from an early age can struggle with imposter syndrome.

Those familiar with the power of the unconscious mind will know its primary aim is to protect us because it does not want us to fail or to look like a fool. The simplest way to avoid failure is to never begin. In its primary desire to give you the best outcome, your own mind can also be the accuser. When you put yourself in the spotlight by starting a business, pursuing education, or starting a relationship, you are opening yourself to the possibility of ridicule, failure, and embarrassment. Wouldn't it just be easier not to bother? You must continue to remember your successes, to build on them, to focus on them. You must also accept failure as a possibility, as a part of the journey, not the ultimate destination.

Your accuser might not be a person. It might be an amalgam of many experiences and beliefs. It could be an observation, the sting of someone else's failure. Passing thoughts like, "I'll never let that happen to me" or "I would die if that happened to me" are often stored in the vault marked "Reasons I will never take a risk." You must be vigilant, learn to recognize the signs, hear the voice, and counter it with your own positive response.

A client struggled to find a job she was happy with and was sabotaging her own attempts at reaching her potential. She was smart and well above average in her intellect. She didn't have an obvious case of imposter syndrome, yet she found it hard to get motivated to move forward in her career. Through an exploration of her personal history, she uncovered some truths that had been buried for many years. A conversation long forgotten suddenly made sense of her situation. She had overheard her parents discussing whether they should spend the money on sending her to college. They were probably only having the conversations that people have in households every day, pondering questions of finance and wondering about the future, yet the way Trudy interpreted it was that they didn't believe she was worth the investment, that she wasn't good enough. That conversation was buried in the unconscious, and though she went to college and succeeded far beyond her expectations, niggling doubts remained. Was it a fluke? Would she fail if she tried to get a job based on her credentials? Had she gone as far as she was likely to go? It seemed easier to sabotage her chances, stay home, and take jobs below her level that she could do with ease, and then there would be no chance of failure.

Ugly Ducklings

When I was around people like me, I was comfortable. When faced with someone who stood out, I wanted to shrink into a corner and avoid being noticed as the ugly duckling that I felt I was.

I had to go re-read the Hans Christian Andersen's fairy tale to jog my memory.

According to the story, an egg finds its way into the wrong nest and hatches, resulting in the birth of an ugly duckling with a face only a mother could love. The other birds bully the duckling because it's different. It's not a duckling at all. It's a baby swan just waiting to transform into its majesty. This is supposed to be a message of transformation, yet I wonder if it's just another story that's been used to make us fit in. When I think of that story now, it makes me sad. The duckling had to become a swan before it could have self-worth. I remember as a child looking at illustrated books and thinking it didn't look too bad, just a little different, torn between the belief that there is hope for us all and the opposite, that we must change and transform ourselves to be accepted. What if you never become a swan? What does that make you?

When I worked as a singer in a band as one of two lead vocalists, I spent a lot of time in comparison mode. My co-singer became my friend, and we are still in contact over thirty years later. It took me a long time to realize that my lack of self-esteem and view of myself affected the way I saw her. If you were to look at a picture, you would likely see two young women, both attractive in their own way. Yet I built her up into the swan compared to my fat ugly duckling self. Through my eyes, everything she wore seemed glamorous and well put together.

She was stylish and knew how to apply makeup to its best effect. I thankfully learned a lot from her, but I viewed her through a lens of comparison, which was unfair to both of us.

Discover Your Origin Story

Our beliefs come from somewhere. We are not born believing that we are not good enough. Discovering where our beliefs came from is a good start. For some of us, it might be obvious. When you recognize negative stories coming from your own thoughts or even said out loud, take a moment to deconstruct them.

Give yourself a few moments and think of who springs to mind when considering the negative words you hear yourself saying or thinking.

If you have experienced trauma or abuse, please do this work with a therapist.

One way we justify avoiding making our own decisions is by convincing ourselves that those people doing all the scary stuff will probably fail. Sometimes we even look for failures to support our unconscious argument that something won't work.

You might convince yourself you are not good enough because:

- No one you know has ever done it.
- No one in your family has ever amounted to anything.
- You don't have the experience.
- You have failed in other areas, so why will this be different?
- You don't finish things.
- You are better with structure.
- You work best in a team; you won't make it on your own.

- Your brain doesn't work like that.
- You have only ever done …
- You didn't do well in school.
- You took x number of times to pass your exam.
- No one will like you.
- It's arrogant to believe you are good enough.
- Only the special few are capable.

And now let's consider ways you have decided that everyone else is crazy to do it—whatever "it" is:

Three out of four businesses / relationships / fitness plans fail.
Whatever the current number, that means there is also a number that succeeds.
There are too many people doing it already.
There is always room for another, because you will do it in your unique way.
X did it and they lost everything.
You are your own person, and what is true of others may not be true of you.

> You have been your own critic, and now you must transform yourself into your best cheerleader.

Tall Poppies and Envy

In 2016 the then British Prime Minister, Theresa May, was criticized for her choice of leather pants that cost more than a thousand dollars. I have to clarify that I mean American pants, which Brits call trousers. (British pants are underwear or knickers—confused yet? Now that would have been a lot of money to spend on underwear!) The price of the prime minister's pants likely wouldn't have been a news story in the United States, where politicians are not generally critiqued on the price of their wardrobes. But in the UK, where the government was implementing money-saving austerity measures, May's pants were sending the wrong signal. The British are less comfortable talking about money and wealth than most people, and they often see it as crass. Brits are also sometimes guilty of engaging in tall poppy syndrome.

The origins of the tall poppy story are found in Greek mythology. King Herodotus discovered that killing the powerful was a way of staying in control. The concept of tall poppy syndrome is more focused on lopping off the heads of those who dare to stand out—the tall poppies. It's about envy and its evil twin jealousy. We can't bear to see others doing well because it shines a light on our own feelings of inadequacy. It's easier to tear them down than face our own lack of commitment to success and ultimate failure to launch.

Our modern imposter syndrome might be connected to tall poppy syndrome. We use excuses to avoid taking the steps to success. If you say any of the following, then check yourself:

Well, it's easier for her because.
He's always had all the breaks.
With that background, he would always find it easier to succeed.

Although some begin with a better chance of success, even if the playing field is not even, that does not mean we should use it as an excuse not to get started. Excuses are where our dreams die. We must look at what we can learn from the tall poppies instead of lopping them off at the head.

Envy makes it difficult to be successful because it's based in fear and a feeling of lack rather than abundance. When we are envious of others, we can't feel good about their successes because it reflects on what we don't have. We cut ourselves off from the possibility of our own desire as we look sideways at the gifts our frenemies enjoy. If only we could see that rejoicing in the happiness and goodness of other people's lives is the key to unlocking our own abundance. I don't speak about this without genuine empathy for anyone who suffers from it. I know myself well enough to catch my own white lies.

Decades ago, I felt powerful envy of another singer. I wasn't performing regularly. There was no good reason except that I hadn't got my ass in gear and made it happen. I remember seeing this woman perform and it was almost a physical pain—

it should have been me. I know how petulant that sounds and I only tell you because I know if you have experienced this feeling; you know how awful it feels. The beneficial part of this story is that the experience spurred me into action, I got back where I needed to be, and sang again. I had no ill will towards the singer and thought she was amazing. I just knew that I should have been on a stage as well and seeing her reminded me I wasn't. There was room for both of us, and it wasn't a competitive issue. When I sang again, I could finally enjoy watching others perform. My envy was in some ways useful in that it made me uncomfortable enough to make a change and spurred me to take action.

When we allow our fear-based envy to become dangerous, it can increase the possibility of self-sabotage. In extreme circumstances, when it is more jealousy than a benign form of envy, it can destroy friendships and even cause the holder to behave badly. A good antidote to envy is gratitude. When we consider all that we have to be grateful for, it often has the power to wash away feelings of lack. I also find it useful to look at others and ask myself some honest questions.

Would I want their life?
Would I be prepared to do what they have done, to have what they have?
What could I do to get closer to achieving what they have?

I have not yet found a person with whom I would want to trade lives. I remember hearing about a celebrity who had signed a deal to perform at one of the big casinos in Las Vegas. The contract was for five years. I was at the time enjoying singing in small pubs and clubs. The distance between me and that superstar singer seemed like a million miles. I thought about what it would be like to do the same show every night for years and shuddered. Millions of dollars, glamorous clothes, and adoring fans would not have made that job appealing to me because it would be so lacking in freedom. I knew I would always prefer my local restaurant with a free pizza thrown in. When we want something, it's possible we can have it if we are prepared to work hard. Success might not look the same for you as it does for someone else.

Maybe You Just Don't Want to Do It

A top violin player might have to practice for up to sixteen hours a day. Are you willing to give that level of commitment to achieve your dreams? When we do work that we are passionate about, it's possible to get into a flow state and time melts away, yet success also requires hard work even if you don't love what you do. Facing your imposter syndrome means picking apart the strands of truth that are not always clear.

Imposter syndrome is about:

- Not believing in yourself.
- Fearing that they will find you out.
- Believing that you are a fraud.
- Believing everyone is better than you.

It is not making a choice not to do something that other people think you should do. How do you know the difference? Sometimes we don't know what we want until we try it out. We might dream of a career, a hobby, a vacation, or trip and discover that it is not what we imagined or what we want to do.

We might have spent a lifetime being prepared for a certain life, never questioning whether it's what we want. In a career or family business, it can be confusing to untangle what we want from what is expected of us. When others are involved in the decision or influence us, we might not know for sure what we want. What have you always thought you would do if there was nothing to stop you? If you were good enough?

Separate People from Their Behavior

When you get annoyed, irritated, or angry with someone who sees the world differently from you, it wastes your energy, takes away your positivity and blocks the good stuff from flowing to you. Imagine for a moment someone says something nasty, mean, or negative to you and you are ready to react. Take a moment to look at them, deep inside, and imagine:

Their Mom just died.
They found out they had cancer.
Their child was missing.
They have just lost their job.
They are sad, angry, and unhappy for a million reasons.
They are normally very nice.
Could you let it go?

Learning from Narcissists

There are some circumstances where too much self-esteem and confidence are not healthy. I'm talking about narcissists, those individuals who love themselves so much that their needs are the only ones of any importance. I mention them only because we can learn something from them. It's worth reiterating that most people at some point will have feelings of low self-esteem and lack of confidence—except the narcissist. If you are here because you struggle with it, congratulations, you are probably not a narcissist!

Narcissistic Traits:

1. They love themselves.
2. They believe they are always right.
3. They believe they are better than everyone else.
4. They don't care what people think about them.
5. If you think something negative about them, you are the one in the wrong.
6. They like to do things their own way, break the rules even if it is to the detriment of others.
7. They are charming.
8. They are good at causing a ruckus.
9. They get people to do things for them.

That's a damning list, and maybe you can't imagine what you could learn from it. Look again. If you switch some of these traits to a more positive slant, you might see that they could benefit you.

1. If you want to be confident, practice self-love and try to love others.
2. Believing you are right is necessary to be successful— just make sure you take some counsel. It's OK to get another person's opinion and advice if you are not sure. If someone you trust says you are wrong, be prepared to listen.
3. You can believe you are equal without feeling superior.
4. It's OK to disregard other's opinions when you are going after your goals, but make sure you are kind and respectful.
5. Breaking the rules can be especially helpful when you are attempting to do groundbreaking work. You do

not have to break the law, hurt other people, or be rude.

6. Charm is good. Manipulation, not so much. Make sure you are being genuine in your charm offensive.

7. We all need to shake things up sometimes, it's often vital in business. People shouldn't leave a meeting with you feeling that you are dangerous, mean spirited or untrustworthy. It is vital that you consider people's feelings and be sensitive to how your behavior impacts others.

8. If you have expectations that people will do things for you, remember the law of reciprocity, people are more likely to do things for people who have helped them.

9. Remember also to avoid manipulation.

Have you ever had someone say you shouldn't do something because it's risky, dangerous, not a good idea? Or many reasons why whatever adventure you are about to embark upon is not wise? Before this happens again, I want you to take a step back and consider the time it happened before.

- Who was the messenger?
- Was it someone you trust?
- Was it someone you normally take advice from?
- Does the person know anything about the adventure you were about to embark on?
- Are they someone who takes less or more risks than you?
- Are they a competitor?
- Are they usually supportive?
- Have they ever encouraged you or anyone you know?
- Do you think they have your best interests at heart?
- Do they believe in themselves?

Others can discourage us from following our dreams because they are afraid to follow their own. It may not be a conscious decision to discourage you or have you doubt yourself. When we have a lack of confidence in our convictions, it doesn't take much to knock us down. Always question the source of advice and their potential motives. Your willingness to take a risk shines a hard light on other's lack of confidence in their own abilities. Again, they may not be purposefully jeopardizing your success, they may struggle with their own self-worth and project that onto you.

Instead of listening to the naysayers, surround yourself with cheerleaders, find people who you admire and who are really pushing themselves. Join a group of inventors, entrepreneurs, athletes, runners, writers, artists, or anyone who will encourage you to push rather than limit yourself. You know what happens when you spend time with people who are smart, daring, and adventurous? Their behavior looks normal. If we are the average of the five people that we spend the most time with, then we should make sure we are with the smart ones. If you feel like everyone in the room knows more than you, good! Then there is something you can learn. The other thing about smart people, especially people who have already reached a level of success, they want to share it; they want to encourage you to grow. Find a mentor, someone who will push you and hold you accountable.

2

DO YOU KNOW WHAT EVERYONE CALLS YOU?

I can see myself dancing like no one was watching. Unfortunately, they were.

I knew I wasn't the best looking, and in fact, I had very little confidence in the way I looked. Yet I can still remember the words spoken about me over four decades ago. I had left school with little of a plan; I worked in a relatively dull job during the day and lived for the weekends where I had found a place in the clubs and pubs, dancing to my favorite bands. It wasn't a dressy scene; the uniform was jeans, T-shirts, and hippie-type skirts. At about ten pounds heavier than the most popular girls, I dreamed of being skinny. In my mind, the extra pounds set me apart for ridicule.

Today I'm sure I could look back at photographs and see a young woman who looked perfectly fine, but back then I struggled terribly and constantly compared myself to others.

Do you know what everyone calls you?

The question came from a mean boy rather than a mean girl. I knew him outside of the clubs, and he often told me I didn't measure up and that I should wear more make-up like the other girls. I didn't reckon on him being in my safe place—the club where I drank and partied on the weekend. That night I was alone on the dance floor enjoying a favorite song in a world of my own. I noticed him and his friends and tried not to think they were watching me.

The next week when I saw him, he asked the question that would continue to haunt me. "Do you know what everyone calls you?"

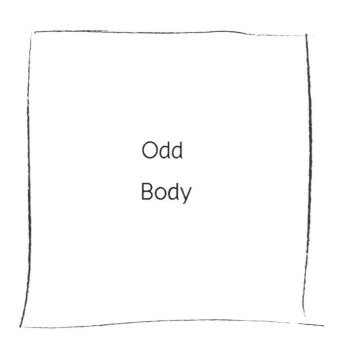

Odd Body

Odd body! It made complete sense. That weekend I had worn my faded jeans that were a little low slung paired with a green cap sleeve T-shirt that was a shiny material and hugged my belly that hung a little over the jeans. *Odd Body*. Yep, that summed me up. I was disgusting. I had kidded myself that I looked cool and that I fit in when I looked gross.

I didn't feel like an imposter when I was dancing like no one was watching, yet when they were not only watching but judging me harshly, it devastated me. Cruel words can have lasting effects. Shortly after that conversation, I started my futile journey through hundreds of pointless diets and miracle weight-loss plans.

That boy's criticism took me back to my school days when I felt judged on everything. When I said that my family was relatively poor, I am not saying it in a woe-is-me kind of way. It was a reality. We had less in material terms than many others, and yet we also had much more in other ways. We were a strong family; we were loved, and we were happy. We didn't have nice furniture, never went on vacations, and as kids, we rarely had nice clothes. My mum was skilled at sewing and knitting and made us clothes with love that today you would pay a fortune for, yet back then we just wanted to look like everyone else.

Hand-Me-Down Memories

I get a feeling of excitement when I buy something new, and it has that "new purse smell." Some of you like the new car smell, and it's not really the smell you like, it's the symbolism, the thrill of owning something shiny and brand new. When I am sad, angry, bereaved, or desperate, I go shopping. It's my happy place. As kids we didn't get new things often, and anything new was exciting, so it clouded my judgment. If there was something that I could own that was unworn by someone else, I wanted it, and this became the cause of some embarrassment. Why did it have to be new? We often got hand-me-downs, donated from other families, or I might get something from my older sister.

While my friends get excited about buying bargains from thrift stores, it's a hard no with me. If you'd grown up wearing clothes from an unfamiliar household that held smells you could not put your finger on, that is not an experience you want to take into adulthood. One particularly memorable batch of donated clothes included some embarrassingly dated leggings, the kind that had stirrups to hook under your feet—before they later came back into fashion. I had the genius idea of chopping off the elastic and expected that they would magically transform into the more fashionable ones without stirrups. You are ahead of me, right? The elastic was the only thing stopping them from riding halfway up my leg. It left me with a pair of used, out-of-style pants that looked like high waters. On this occasion, my mum took pity on me and didn't make me wear them. I was also regularly covered in cat hair from our white and black cat. I loved him, but he made looking well-groomed almost impossible. I was recently feeding my friend's cats and went to the grocery store on the way home. A man approached me and asked, "Cat or dog?" I was unaware that I had collected a portion of their hair during the visit. It reminded me of the scruffy kid with cat hair on her school uniform.

Bargain Embarrassments

New is not always better. On a family shopping trip to the market in my high school years, I learned this the hard way. Browsing in a little store that sold odds and ends. A pair of blue and black shiny shoes captivated me. To this day, I do not understand what I was thinking. All I can tell you is they were 50 pence, the equivalent of two quarters, and they were my size. Because the store was almost giving them away, it blinded me to the reality that they were ridiculous. All I could see was that they were new. I asked my mum to buy them for me; she gave me a sidelong look, and I convinced her they would go with my blue school uniform. She agreed to let me have them. I wore them only once. I became the center of attention for all the wrong reasons, and it could have launched my comedy career if I'd had a routine prepared.

I even had my own theme song. A chorus followed me throughout the day:

"She's wearing clown shoes."

"She's wearing clown shoes."

And that's exactly what they looked like. I convinced myself that they were cool and quirky, but they weren't, and I looked like a fool.

Feeling judged on our appearance does not help our confidence. I have had many opportunities to buy good quality items and instead went with a cheaper option. Poverty mentality and fear of running out of money can add up to terrible choices. Have you ever had that feeling when things are going well? The feeling that something bad will happen and it will soon all fall apart? I was like that with spending money on clothes. The first expensive personal item I bought didn't last long. I was vacationing in Italy and saw a beautiful leather purse. The price was more than I had ever spent on one item before. I decided it would be a wonderful reminder of our vacation and a special treat. I received many compliments, but my enjoyment was short-lived. Someone stole my purse, along with all its contents, just a few weeks later. I then went back to believing it was just not worth having nice things. An imposter would think that, right? Having good quality possessions is not necessarily dependent on how much money we have. If I add up all the junk that I bought as bargains and never wore, I could have had beautiful clothes my entire life. And I know plenty of wealthy people who dress cheaply. I am learning not to judge others or myself on appearances and to choose quality over bargains, or both, if that is possible.

You are learning a little of where my imposter syndrome came from—weight issues, the wrong clothes, never having proper haircuts as kids, and much more. The best is yet to come.

Have you ever experienced the horror of head lice? When everyone else got them at primary school, I avoided them. When I reached high school, I picked them up from my little brother. I tell him that while I was teaching him to read; he was giving me lice! Added to everything else that caused my confidence to plummet was having head lice in high school. I kept it a secret, and it was one of the rare occasions my mum allowed me to stay out of school until we were sure the treatment had worked. I had my long hair cut off to be doubly sure I was clear and spent another few months feeling dirty, scruffy, and not good enough.

Maybe you don't have concerns about the way you look. Maybe you know you look great yet have other areas of your life where the doubt creeps in. Or maybe you are gorgeous and don't know it or don't believe it. Imposter syndrome is not about outward appearances, but the way you feel about how you are perceived and how you see yourself. It can affect overall confidence.

Feeling like an imposter continued throughout my life, affecting many of my choices, my relationships, and many of my decisions. I was never sure what I wanted or liked because I was consumed with self-doubt. If this does not resonate with you, maybe you have never been a people pleaser. I look around now and I see it—people doing things they don't want to do, spending their precious time on activities someone else said were cool or right or because their spouse or friends do it.

Later in the book, I have some ideas for you to help you discover what you enjoy doing. Don't worry that you might become an inconsiderate and selfish person. You won't. You will, however, become less resentful and more confident, happy, and fulfilled.

I Believed I Was Ugly

Trigger warning: If you have feelings about low self-esteem based on the way you look, or have looked in the past, this might upset you. It was difficult to write, yet it's important to recognize that imposter syndrome can stem from the way we perceived ourselves in our childhood.

Look at the picture

Most kids get sent to school looking their best for photo day. (Sadly, this was not the worst one—I just didn't bother to take some of them home.) I'm not trying to shame anyone, least of all my younger self. This was before anyone had heard of the concept of body positivity. I had a terrible haircut, sallow skin—probably from a poor diet and living in a damp house with a dad who smoked heavily—and teeth that looked like they hadn't been brushed in a while. Yet all I could see was my nose. It looked huge to me, and I hated what I saw in the mirror. There wasn't the budget for proper haircuts, and so the wonky fringe just added to my feeling of ugliness and highlighted my big fat nose. This was also around the time puberty hit, and as much as I hated this photo, it was probably the only one where I didn't have pimples for the next three decades.

Hating my looks continued until I was in my thirties when I lost weight and learned a little about makeup. I'm not sharing any of this to solicit pity. Most people probably considered me plain rather than ugly, but it is important to recognize where our feelings of not being good enough come from.

My talent for singing and acting saved me. I was confident in my vocal abilities, and it didn't matter if I didn't get the part of a pretty girl because I would have the better and often more interesting role. They once cast me as a boy, and that didn't bother me either. My fallback position was to say that my looks shouldn't be important because I was playing a part, and that was what mattered. I used this piece of self-deception for a long time before I admitted to myself that I wanted to look attractive and stopped self-sabotaging my chances of looking good.

We must separate this discussion from that of body positivity. How you feel about yourself is what is important. There might be people who remember me from my school days and don't remember an ugly girl who didn't fit in. That is not what is important. How we see ourselves is where our self-esteem comes from. Think about it—it's *self*-esteem, not *what-people-think-about-me*-esteem. There is nothing wrong with making the best of yourself or wanting to make a good impression on those around you. My challenge was that I did not know how to do either of those things. I remember occasionally my mum would put rollers in my hair, and she would tell me that "pride is painful" if I complained. I eventually gave up trying. It is ironic that I joined a subculture of punks and rockers in the mistaken belief that what you wore didn't matter. Of course it mattered. The rules and the uniform were different, but it still mattered.

I am not saying that I spent my childhood crying into my multiple chocolate bars. I had fun teenage years, but I was never happy with the way I looked and did not know how to make it better. For this book, I felt it was important to share some of my background and the pain I felt growing up. I know it is likely not that much different from the way many of you might feel.

Everyone's experience is different and important to them. Undermining their story by believing their experience was not that bad or valid is not helpful. You can't fully understand someone else's experience because you didn't live it. Other people's experiences, particularly during childhood, might be foreign or seem insignificant to you, but they likely had an enormous impact on who that person became. I am no longer the child that felt ashamed of herself, yet sometimes she pops up, and I have to love her and remind her that everything is OK now.

Though we are shaped by our experiences, it doesn't have to stay that way. We can change, though we need to do some work. Now let's focus on you!

3

DO WHAT YOU LIKE AND FIND YOUR PEOPLE

You might be good at something and not enjoy doing it, or there might be things that are just not your thing. That's OK. You do not have to be good at everything. Find what you *want* to do. You might be passionate about it, you might not. The key thing to remember is that *you* get to make the choice.

Have you ever put someone on a pedestal only to discover they are not perfect after all? An author I admire and find inspirational turned out to be a let-down as a presenter. I had bought most of her books and tried one of her online trainings. It did not work for me at all. She didn't come across well; the lighting was all wrong, and the style of training did not connect with me. You know what? I'm sure she doesn't give a toss about my opinions. She's making a ton of money, and this was just one of her many offerings. Similarly, if you look at someone's first product, it probably wasn't very good or not as good as their current stuff. One myth of this world is that you must be a devoted follower of every aspect of celebrities, political parties, and those who you admire. It's much healthier to admit that while you support some of it, you don't agree with all of it, because if you were to like all of it, then it's likely a cult. Dare to have some nuance—like what you like, ignore the rest. It's also healthy to recognize that others likely will feel the same way about you, because not everyone will like you or everything that you do.

You Are Not for Everyone

I didn't watch "Game of Thrones," but I watched "Westworld" three times. We are all different, and I don't get bent out of shape because people don't like the same things I do. There are only so many hours in the day, and I will not spend all of them watching shows so I can talk about them. In this life, you will appeal to the right people, whether that's friends, business associates, clients, or employers. Stop trying to fit in. The world needs what you have, so don't waste your time on those who are not your people. My products and services are not only not for my friends, but they are also not for my husband. Although I think some of what I write would be helpful for him, he doesn't want to hear it from me. There are billions of people in the world, so stop trying to please them all. To be the authentic you, you might even have to upset a few of them. We are often so busy trying to prove that we fit in, that we cannot be the person we could be. It's time for that question again.

What would you do if you weren't afraid?
Before you get to write that down, let's ask another one.
What are you worried that you can't do or won't be able to do?

You Don't Have to See the Whole Picture to Follow Your Dream

Begin! It is all you have to do—one step, one hour, one day at a time. In a particular task, you might not be good enough… yet.

Everyone has to start somewhere.

I would have never believed I could write a book, and here I am on number four. When I begin, I often don't think it will come together. It's just a jumble of words and random thoughts, yet every day I write more, and then I put it into some order to make it make sense. One word, one line at a time. When I wrote my first book, I deleted ten thousand words—around a third of the book. I had to write *something* before I could decide what could stay and what would not make the final edit. Just because we worry we are not good enough doesn't mean we have to be sloppy. As someone once said, you can't edit a blank page.

Do you ever think some people just get there more easily or quickly than you do? Well, maybe they do in some areas of their life. Yet most accomplished people must make a consistent effort, never giving up, not complaining, just doing it. We can't look at other people and decide we are not as good as them if we don't at least try.

Things that look easy but require practice:

- Playing an instrument.
- Being a talented public speaker.
- Being an artist.
- Being accomplished in sports.
- Baking a consistent batch of goods.

Let's look at this one for a minute. I enjoy baking, and I'm good at it. What I mean by this is that I can make something that you will probably enjoy eating (unless you don't eat sugar) and come back for more. I watched a popular baking show that everyone was talking about. The sight of the incredible cakes and biscuits (cookies) made my mouth water. When they explained the rules, I realized that I was not a baker in the same universe as they were. It required them to make each item look the same, perfectly uniform. When I bake my ginger snap cookies, they come in all shapes and sizes, and they always taste good. I don't plan on creating a product based on perfect dimensions. Does that mean I am not good at baking? No. I don't care that mine would not pass a test by a celebrity judge. I am happy with what I can do, and I have no desire to put in any further effort in improving them.

I was fortunate that when I was in a band, I sang rather than played an instrument. Singing is improved by practicing, and while that might require vocal exercises and scales, it's not quite the same as spending multiple hours a day practicing piano. I did, however, become unstuck when I took my voice for granted and did not give it the care and attention that it required. Overuse of my voice, lack of sleep, and occasional smoking led me to damage my vocal cords and required surgery. If I had been playing guitar, I wouldn't have neglected my instrument or allowed it to be damaged. Self-esteem also comes from having respect for ourselves.

You are unique, and that special sauce that you have differs completely from anyone else's. While writing this book, I had one of many moments I have had over the last few years where I wondered what on earth I am doing. Who am I to think I can help anyone? It was a Sunday morning, and I decided not for the first time that I would give it all up. I would see how far I could get by limiting what I do, move away from social media, and just allow myself to retire quietly working in whatever way I could and making my life and my circle smaller and less exhausting. I had planned to go to an event locally and went along feeling less than optimistic. When I arrived, I was immediately welcomed by people I had not seen in a while, multiple people—some of whom I had convinced myself I'd not helped at all—came to me and said that my work had made a positive impact on their lives. The next day I randomly received an email of encouragement from someone I barely know, telling me I was an excellent teacher. This encouragement made me realize I was still running away from my true self and my path. I have a purpose, as do you, and we need to give into it and let it flow as it should.

Do It Your Way

There are a million ways to achieve your goal or follow your dream, and you do not have to do it the same way your friend, sister, father, preacher, teacher, or guru does it. When you suffer from lack of self-esteem or imposter syndrome, you don't always know what you want. If you have spent a lifetime believing that you don't deserve or are not good enough to reach your goals or dreams, you might have scaled down to something more manageable that you believe is possible. If you observe the behavior of successful people, you see that they usually know what they want and are also equally adamant about the things they don't want. They clear a path for their success.

But how do you know what you want? How can you trust your own judgment when it has betrayed you for so long? Begin by questioning your motives. In a world dominated by social media, it's difficult to separate what we want from what we think will impress people. When I order something quirky from a restaurant—deep fried cheesecake, for example, it is popular and gets me likes on social media. Did I really want it? Or did I want the likes? A new restaurant recently opened in our town, and all the cool people were posting about being there. My initial thought was, "We should go there this weekend," and then I thought again. Why? Was it the food I wanted? The more I thought about this, the more I realized how I make choices like this every day without thinking. We ended up going to a restaurant we know and like that had similar food at around half the price. We didn't Instagram our food—just ate it. I then thought of the other areas of my life and whether I know what I want or whether I am being influenced by external factors and trends. I am constantly decluttering my wardrobe, and it's often to get rid of things I bought in error. I rebuy those damn clown shoes over and over. The adult version is beautiful shoes that I can't walk in and just sit in the closet. I am still working on finding the confidence to buy what I like to wear and stick with it.

What do you like? Next time you make a choice, ask yourself, is this just for me? Or is it to impress other people? When you are struggling with confidence issues, you will be less likely to do things right for you. This is true for your career, your hobbies, the clothes you wear and the food you eat. If you could start with one thing that you normally do to please others, what would change if you were to do it the way you want?

I recently experimented with bright colors in my hair, initially adding a few purple tints to switch things up, I then added more and couldn't decide if I liked them or not. I originally did it to please me. I had almost decided I was over it when someone criticized the color. And this is where rebellious Trish surfaced—not that the person who made the snarky comment was someone whose views I respected. I refuse to have anyone tell me what to do, and for that reason I almost stayed with something I no longer wanted. I had to think long and hard about what I wanted and not what I was trying to prove. I realized I didn't love the color. I had it taken out and instantly felt better. I encourage you to experiment. How will you know what you like if you are afraid to step away from what you have always done?

Am I teaching you to be selfish? Possibly, because putting yourself first for a change will be helpful in figuring out what you want and achieving your goals.

4

LIES YOU HAVE TOLD YOURSELF

Sometimes the reason we aren't succeeding or thriving, or even surviving, is self-sabotage. One of the most common ways we self-sabotage is by believing our own lies. When we give those lies credence, it's easier to believe that we are not good enough, and that naturally provides us with the perfect excuse not to do anything at all.

Starting scared is still starting. It doesn't matter if our efforts aren't perfect or even if moving forward feels uncomfortable and unfamiliar—forward movement is the key. It really doesn't matter—just do something. Let's say you want to exercise. There's no magic formula. Put one foot in front of the other and walk around the block, up the stairs or to the far corner of the store parking lot. Just start moving. I once ran a marathon; it started with a slow run, increasing every week until I reached twenty-six miles. When I think of it today, I still can barely believe it as I don't do those distances now, but everyone starts with that single step.

Maybe you want to write a book. Start with a title, a single character, or a brief story. Brainstorm, research, read about your topic, and keep writing. Eventually you will hit a groove. Are you thinking you might want a new job? Start looking. Go online and see what's being posted. Brush up your résumé, buy a new outfit, spread the word among trusted friends and colleagues, and believe that it will happen soon.

Remember the child who was daring and confident, who was afraid of nothing and believed that she could do anything? That child is still in there, and pops up now and then, trying to have fun before getting crushed by responsibilities, fear, and other people's expectations. Allow the child you once were to come out to play. Let your creativity flow!

The Power of Words

Have you ever had one of those dreams where you find yourself at work or in a social situation, and to your horror, you discover you are naked? Even in a dream, it's the worst feeling. That's what imposter syndrome can feel like, as if everyone is looking at you, and you are without the protection of not just your clothes but your skills. Being naked of our protective layer, being seen as we really are, not how we want people to see us, is terrifying.

Do you know the power of your words? When you tell yourself stories that are not true, your unconscious mind believes them. Your beliefs also can make you sick. You curse yourself by repeating lies. Here's what some of these common lies sound like:

I could never do that.
I'm not strong enough.
I'm no good at this.
I always mess up.
It always goes wrong for me.
I don't deserve this.

It's too late.
I'll always be fat/sick/unwell/tired.

Listen to your language, and the next time you catch yourself speaking lies, stop and turn the lies into statements you might say to a friend or loved one.

You can do it.
You are strong enough.
You are good at this.
You can succeed.
It will go right this time.
You deserve this.
You still have time.

Many of you are doing amazing work, achieving things others could only dream of, and still you don't believe in your own abilities. Do any of these thoughts sound familiar?

Anyone could have done it.
I only succeeded because I did a lot of reading.
I only completed it because of all the resources available to me.
I was just lucky this time.
I got a lot of help.
I made it up as I went along.
It was a fluke.
The competition wasn't very good.
I chose the easiest so I would get through.
I probably can't replicate what I did.
Yes, but.

These are the excuses we tell ourselves when we are not prepared to take credit for our success and achievements. The truth is no one does anything alone, everyone has help, and we all have good and bad days. Take the compliment, claim your achievement, and believe that you are worthy.

When I joined a training group to run that marathon, I was told that we were part of a small group, a tiny percentage of the population who would ever do it. When I struggled and wondered why I, as one of the slowest runners, should even bother, I reminded myself of that message. Even if I was slower than everyone in my group, I was still out there doing something that over ninety-nine percent of the population would never even try. Taking action is the first step, second guessing, and judging ourselves is not helpful. We cannot get better if we do not start. We cannot improve our running speed if we are lying in bed. We cannot edit an empty page, and we cannot begin a relationship by hiding from potential mates. Anything we want to achieve will require action, and that first step is often the scariest.

When I was working with those looking for employment, it was sad to learn some people believed they weren't good at anything. This was especially true of women returning to the workforce after bringing up children. They would discount all the skills they had learned and developed while doing one of the most important jobs of all. It was my job to show them they had transferable skills that were also valuable in the workplace. Whether that is you or you are not sure what skills you have, it is worth taking an inventory. Think about what other people say about you. What do they say you are good at? What do they praise you for? Building a list of these observations is a great way to build your confidence. Consider some of these:

- Cook
- Driver
- Navigator
- Artist
- Bargain hunter
- Negotiator
- Peacemaker
- Gift chooser
- Painter
- Interior designer
- Healthcare worker
- Nurse
- Therapist
- Coach
- Handyperson
- Plumber
- Electrician
- Gardener
- Cheerleader
- Encourager
- Pet sitter
- Add your own...

Look at any of these roles and consider the skills required to do the job. Now see all the ways you add value to people's lives and all you can do. That is worth celebrating and recognizing. You are unique, and we need your skills, even if you might not have found your niche yet. If you keep waiting, there might come a time when it will be harder to get started than right now. You are smart enough. If you can read, then you can learn. If there is something you don't know how to do, there are people willing to show you or a YouTube video that can demonstrate it. This is the perfect time to do that thing you want to do and remember—there is no such thing as failure. You just try another way until you figure it out.

The Power of Social Media

Another thing that is likely is making your imposter syndrome worse is the time and focus that you spend on social media. Everyone is apparently eating gorgeous food, dining at expensive restaurants, wearing the best clothes, and visiting exotic locations with their gorgeous significant others, right? Wrong. When I go to a restaurant and the food is good, I have eaten half of it before I even think to take a picture. When I see those photos, I usually want to yell, "Put your damn phone away and eat your food!" If you are already feeling like you are not good enough, gazing at other people's perfectly posed images—which are all carefully designed to convey they are out there living their best lives—is unlikely to make you feel better.

Some of my smartest, most accomplished friends never post their achievements online. They are too busy making things happen. You also will not know the truth about another's success by believing everything you see online. It's not necessarily a lie, but you can bet it's been varnished and tweaked to making it just a little shinier. They say you can't polish a turd, yet you can do a suitable job of molding a pile of poop into something more attractive. When I first started in business, I couldn't figure out why everyone else was on the way to becoming a millionaire when they had only just started, and I wasn't exactly rolling in the dough. I finally learned that they weren't all making tons of money. They were just creating that illusion, hoping everyone would buy into the idea that they were successful and make it true. I'm not saying we shouldn't be aspirational, yet if faking it till you make it means working sixteen hours a day pretending you are living it large while you are struggling to pay your bills, it might be time to get real.

If you compare yourself to the overnight successes that really aren't, you will end up disappointed and depressed. When I finally said in a mastermind group that I was tired of working so hard and not getting anywhere, things changed. I realized what I was doing wasn't working. I was open to ideas and change, and I knew I was a hard worker, so I resolved to try something else. After that decision, I got opportunities that took me in a slightly different direction and opened up new avenues for success. The next time you see someone post on social media and wonder how they are suddenly a hit when they have been doing it for all of five minutes, accept that you might not be seeing the whole picture. Maybe there has been build up you haven't seen, or maybe they have a lot of support, and you are only seeing a small part of the story. Maybe they are bullshitting, and none of it is true.

I was recently approached by someone offering to make me a bestselling author—hey, did they not see I already am? (more on that later). I normally dismiss these pitches out of hand, yet as I was leading workshops on self-publishing and encouraging participants to recognize scammers, I thought a little research would be helpful. Although I won't say the person was a scammer, they had some impressive glossy information and said all the right things. I did what any self-respecting sceptic would do. I went to Amazon and looked at their book sales. As I had suspected, they had quite a low ranking, and all evidence pointed to the fact that they weren't selling many books. If someone tells me they can make me a best seller, but they can't sell their own books, maybe they are not being transparent about their success. The bestseller thing is a game. I have been a bestseller in several categories at various times on Amazon, and it doesn't always represent a massive number of sales. Sometimes it's because I am discounting a book, sometimes it's because the category is small and I only need to sell a handful of books to reach best-seller status, and sometimes it's because I am giving it away for free. Yes, you can be a bestseller making no money. I am also approached by people who want to give me products for free, so I will give them a five-star review. Not everything is as it appears, and you might be comparing yourself to an illusion. How can you measure up to something that doesn't really exist?

There is nothing wrong with showing your best self. Heck, I don't want you to see me without makeup, so I guess that's false advertising too, though I'm not telling you I have the secret of eternal youth or offering beauty tips!

Just remember that you are good enough and compare yourself only with the you of yesterday. Aspire to be better, model positive behavior, and question what you see. I have spent time on TV sets and in recording studios. I have spent days recording a song to get the vocals perfect. I have had my photograph taken on a TV set to make sure my make-up looks exactly the same when taking a break to ensure continuity, and that is just as an extra on TV shows. You are more than good enough.

5

MINDSET MATTERS

You can do all the preparation in the world—get a mentor, hire a fitness trainer, consult experts, and read all the right books—yet if you don't change your mindset, you are wasting your time.

We get what we focus on, and that includes all the bad stuff. If you constantly think about everything that could go wrong and all the reasons you won't be successful, happy, and fulfilled, you will get more of that. Our unconscious minds do not understand the difference between what is real and imagined. I imagine that you have heard this before, but have you truly taken it on board? What do you allow your mind to focus on? There is a good reason successful people do affirmations and talk positively about themselves. They are programming their brain to believe the good stuff along with taking positive action. If you are in the habit of thinking negatively and have become used to the negative programming, you will need to do some extra positive reinforcement. We will use simple methods to help you reprogram and reboot your brain, so it prepares you for success. It doesn't matter what your goal is, whether it's education, career, relationships, or health.

I regularly see posts about Mercury in retrograde. The belief that the alignment of the planets can affect us negatively. Apparently, this phenomenon makes all our electrical stuff go to crap. I am not debating or debasing anyone's belief; however, it is important to consider that the more you believe bad things will happen, the more likely they will. Mercury is in retrograde multiple times during the year. I'm sure many of you, as I do, have technical issues inside and outside of these times. It is possible that we are speaking calamities into existence by focusing on them.

Are you ready to talk only positively about yourself? It is vital to fight the imposter within you. There is so much evidence that what we think about, we bring about, and you can go back to my first book, *Why Am I Scared?* to learn more about the power of the unconscious mind.

Confident and successful people constantly speak with surety and a sense of belief, even when things are not going their way. There is no room for doubt. Although politicians can be annoying and might not be the best example, they exhibit a confidence even when they are facing catastrophe. We rarely see leaders with their heads hanging, saying, "Oh, I don't think I can do this. It won't work. I'm not good enough."

To exhibit a positive, confident attitude, we need to behave as if we believe it. Behave like you mean it. Turn your negativity into a positive can-do attitude. If you don't think you are good enough, you are unlikely to be showing other people your best side. Although there are those who are struggling on the inside and no one would know, there are also those who are making it clear they don't have confidence in themselves. You might have to begin with a little pretending, even if it's telling yourself that you deserve to be good enough. What if you were switched at birth and realized that you were born into a wealthy and influential family and now you are about to get your inheritance? I bet you would think about yourself differently, walk a little taller, have higher expectations of the way others treat you. Nothing would have changed other than the story you tell yourself. It's time to write yourself a new, improved story.

Listen to Your Cheerleaders

We are going to model the behavior of a successful, powerful, confident person. Begin by imagining that you have a team of people cheering you on. They are with you every step of the way, ready to encourage you and remind you how amazing you are. Envision that team of people and give them uniforms, voices, and faces. Who would they look like and sound like? Create a powerful and positive virtual team that will always stand ready to encourage you.

What will they say if you ever claim that you are not good enough? What will they do to be sure you are always feeling on top of your game? Begin by thinking of the words you want your cheerleaders to say. They are a part of you, and they need to give you the right words. It might help to think of the negative words you have said in the past and then turn them into what your cheerleaders would say to you to make you feel powerful and positive.

Let's start with the easy ones:
I can't do it.
Yes, you absolutely can do it.
They will figure out I'm not good enough.
You are confident in your abilities.
What if I make a fool of myself and let everyone down?
You will feel so good when you do a good job and make everyone proud.
No one in my family has ever…
How wonderful it will be when you are the first to do…
I once failed and felt stupid.

The next time you will succeed and feel amazing.
I tried once before and it didn't work.
You are so much more confident this time and ready to succeed.
I'm not sure if I have it in me.
You have everything you need to succeed.
There are so many people better than me who are further along.
You will be an inspiration to everyone else who started later and still did well.

From this moment on, you must focus only on good things, on your goals, and your dreams. When you encounter problems or roadblocks, see them as opportunities. Get creative and use problems solved as proof that you are on the right track. Learning to step back and look at things without emotion will help you get to solutions faster. When presented with a problem, imagine you are looking at it through a screen, watching the other version of you that has the problem through a two-way mirror, yet you also have the power to change the behavior. What would you advise that version of you to do? If there was no anger, frustration, or sadness, what would be the simplest option to fix the problem? We create many of our problems by spending time on the way we feel about them, or the way other people have made us feel. No one can make us feel anything. It is our choice how we react. We must train ourselves to react differently and to choose the way we feel. When we do that, then we are empowered and give ourselves every chance to achieve our goals. You must tell yourself a new story, and you must listen only to your cheerleaders. When the negative voices attempt to chime in, you will be ready with a powerful and positive response.

If you have had a lifetime of telling yourself that you can't do it, practice and be diligent. Your cheer team will get stronger as you listen and follow their advice and believe their positive messages.

Be Mindful of Mixed Messages

Sometimes we can accept that we are good at one thing and lack confidence in another. Sometimes we believe in ourselves at the start, only to fall victim to our doubts later on the journey. Often this happens when we are getting close to our goals. We doubt ourselves just as we are ready to cross the finish line. This is normal. We can push down the feelings of self-doubt for only so long and then self-sabotage kicks in and we are back to the feeling that we can't do it. Pushing through and remembering past successes is a good way to remind ourselves that we can do it.

Everyone's pain point is unique, and pain can compel the sufferer to seek help or embrace change when it becomes too much to bear. Those dealing with imposter syndrome may continue with the status quo for a long time after their choices have become uncomfortable. For some, life might well be uncomfortable, but they're convinced they can't be fixed and aren't prepared to change.

I know a thing or two about this. I didn't wait until I was thirty-three to pass my driving test because I was lazy. I worried about failing. I worried I might be one of those people who was still trying to pass after fifty tests, the people they make documentaries about. Thankfully, it was only five!

The concern that we will be the only one who can't do it can infect our thinking so much that it stops us from even trying. Some students get so stressed in exams that their minds go blank and they can't find the answers to the questions even though they have learned them. Self-sabotage is real and yet we rarely realize that we are doing it.

No More Excuses

Imagine this is your last chance to do something you have always wanted to accomplish. Are you going to recite all the reasons it won't work and accept disappointment and regret? Or will you finally choose to believe that much of the scary and seemingly impossible stuff is entirely *possible*? The older I get, the more I learn that the most powerful limits are those that we put on ourselves. Here are few strategies to enact when you start feeling yourself reaching for a familiar, worn-out excuse:

Surround Yourself with Those Who Support You

If you regularly spend time with people who feel bad about themselves and celebrate negative thinking, did I say celebrate? Yes, that's what it is for some. They love misery and misery loves company, so they try to drag you down with them. Limit your exposure to those who are negative. When we are working on ourselves, we don't need people who will pull us down.

Keep a List of Your Achievements

Big and small, anything you have done, that you once didn't think that you could. Building a bank of positive experiences gives you something to draw upon for those times when your confidence is in deficit.

Say Positive Affirmations

There is a trend for women to compliment other women by calling them a queen. If you are a man reading this, I'm not sure there is a comparison. People don't build you up by telling you, you are a king, do they? I don't want to be a queen. I'm from England, and I see what a tough job it is. Queens are not allowed to have an opinion, and they must practice diplomacy about everything. They have no actual power and everywhere they go there is the smell of fresh paint. Queens are also born into their role. They can't change, are tied to tradition, and doing things the way they have always been done.

You know what's better than being a queen? You, but even better, you and the way you want to be—stronger, more confident, more powerful. You have all you need. It just needs coaxing out of you. When I say transformation, I am talking about doing the best with what you have, learning to believe in yourself, and getting better at it every day.

If that means wearing an imaginary crown and imagining your subjects bowing down and curtseying to you, go for it. That just didn't work for me. Your transformation starts with your mind and your attitude. If there is something you have been wanting to do but haven't because you feel you are not good enough, it's time to build your resilience. Whatever you decide you can't do, you must learn to believe that you can. You are in control. No one else will make this happen for you, and there is no one who can stop you.

Sign up for it. A race, a class, a job application.

I had an idea for this book, yet unsure about the concept and felt that I wasn't good enough. Ha-ha, I know. When I was tempted to give up, I hired my editor and cover designer. Accountability will get your butt in gear better than anything. I have signed up for conferences that scared me and trips that I wasn't sure I dared take. Once you are committed it's much harder to give up and believe in the lie that you can't do it.

The way to prove to yourself that you can do it and you are good enough is to do things you think you can't and stretch yourself even further.

6

QUIT OVERTHINKING AND TRYING TO BE PERFECT

I'm an over-thinker and occasional perfectionist. I've even been known to overthink my perfectionism because I'm not convinced that I'm good enough to call myself a perfectionist. Perfectionism is being superb at everything, isn't it? No, actually. Perfectionists often procrastinate, worry, and vacillate back and forth before making a decision. Perfectionism and overthinking are part of the same issue. Some very successful people I know are good at getting things done quickly, however they sometimes make mistakes, and some of their work can be a little sloppy.

I also know people who are very successful and take their time. People tell me I'm productive and that I execute well. This is true, however what they don't see is how long I spend on getting something right. I can spend hours crafting an email because it doesn't sound right. I can spend an equal amount of time looking at a social media post before I comment, because I don't want to offend somebody. I might type the same sentence many times because I'm not sure it quite hits the mark and then delete it and do nothing. When my first book was published, I didn't read the print version as I was too afraid of finding mistakes. I left it for months and when I finally read it; I found a few, and while they weren't major errors, I was horrified. Today that wouldn't bother me so much because I have learned to accept that everything is flawed. I could have waited and chosen not to publish that book, but then I wouldn't have helped people because I worried about periods or a missing word. I still believe in doing my best and double checking my work, yet when we are checking things to the detriment of our productivity or mental health, it's time to look at our reasons.

People rarely care about the things you worry about. Everyone is so busy getting on with their own lives that they don't spend their time losing sleep or writing to the media about the fact that you spelled a word wrong in your book, in a Facebook post, or in a text, or that you forgot to wish somebody a happy birthday. Let's talk about that for a minute. Let's look at a list of my worries and see if any of them sound like you and then let's decide that we will not do this any longer.

Worried that you:

- Made a mistake.
- Said the wrong thing.
- Wore the wrong thing.
- Bought the wrong gift.
- Didn't complement them on the food.
- Said no to something.

Some of you are spending an enormous amount of your personal time buying gifts for family members, worrying yourselves sick about whether it's the right thing or how you'll be judged. Where is the joy in that? Gift giving is supposed to be fun. It's not about one-upmanship or proving something.

I finally became overwhelmed and ultimately stopped sending Christmas cards except to a small group of friends I don't see often and who are primarily overseas. I'd given myself a huge stress about it. I realize it's something that we've always done in our family. My mum used to send out almost one hundred Christmas cards, many to people who she could barely remember. The cost, time, and effort were significant. If you enjoy something and it is not stressing you, that's fine, but if you are doing it because you think you should, it's time to stop and rethink it.

It's usually women tasked with the gift giving. If you are buying gifts on behalf of your significant other for their family and it becomes stressful, have a conversation about changing the process. You are not your significant other's personal shopper, so unless buying gifts for others is your passion, don't do it. Most of the time, we over-thinkers and perfectionists do things because we put the pressure on ourselves rather than it being other people forcing their will on us. Not caring what people think about you is an ongoing challenge. You will never reach the point where you don't care at all what people think, however you can come to realize the futility of such worry.

When I initially came to the United States, I didn't work for a while. There seemed to be a misconception that I had nothing to do and would be interested in attending parties and buying lots of direct sales products. I am not a fan of this sales model. I know I might have offended people, but that is my personal value. I am an aspirational minimalist who prefers to consume less and therefore I will risk offending by saying no to parties or trying your new product line. It took a while to reach this point. I have bought the candles, the jewelry, the cleaning products, the health bars, the cloths, and the purses that were often unused and eventually given to charity even when I couldn't afford them. Now unless it's something I really want, I say no.

Thanks to social media, we can easily be inundated with invitations to events both real world and virtual. Gone are the times when there is nowhere to go and nothing to do. You are unlikely to be the only one receiving the invitation, and the organizer of the event might have invited everybody on their friends list.

I have a particular aversion to invitations masquerading as parties or coffee dates. I'm not sure what some think, but a party is not a party if you're only inviting me because you want me to buy something from you. Call it a launch or call it something else, but don't tell me it's a party when all it is, is the opportunity to buy the latest product you are selling.

Why Don't They "Like" My Stuff?

Here are some truths about social media that you might not know. You've probably seen the posts floating around—myths that Facebook only shows your posts to twenty-seven people, and if you follow their random instructions, say the name Mark Zuckerberg three times in front of a candle while burning incense you will become instantly popular, or some such nonsense that your aunt keeps sharing.

The truth is much simpler. Social media works on engagement. The algorithm (not a person) is constantly guessing what it thinks you want to see, and when you click like and share or *engage*, it gives you more of that. If you never connect with someone, then don't expect that they will see your posts. There is always that chance you are or in the past have been annoying and you have been *unfollowed* or *snoozed*. Or maybe you posted something political or controversial, and your friends might agree with you but don't feel safe to like or comment because they don't want to be associated with the content publicly. If you post some amazing idea, or good news and don't get a lot of likes, it's probably not personal. Our friends like our stuff because they like us. There is also the proximity effect—as we move away from people physically or metaphorically, they are less invested to stay connected. Social media is a never-ending scroll of the good, the bad, and the ugly. If you post something dramatic, tragic, or heartwarming, you will probably get lots of engagement and the more people respond, the more people will see it. If you post an angry political rant, some will ignore you, and those who are supportive might agree with you. Facebook or whatever platform you're on could also say, "Meh, that's not very interesting," and hide it from many of your followers. If you want engagement, engage. If you never message or call your friends, you will go off their radar, and the same goes with social media. Throw out some love to get some back.

Social media also offers the opportunity to overthink in novel ways. Take something as simple as "liking" a post. There was a time when you could only like, but now you can like, love or be angry or sad. What's the correct one? If I like and everyone else loves, does that make me a bad person? Will they judge me? Should I go back and change it? I'm British, so love sometimes feels like too much gushing. And the tragic posts, they are fraught with overthinking opportunities. Is a sad face the only option? If I love it, does that mean I love that someone died when I mean I am sending you love? What if I hit the wrong one? What if I laugh when I meant sad and then I will become a shamed internet meme? What if I forget to say something or what if I say too much? What if I'm too familiar or use a word that doesn't translate culturally? I think I will just pretend I've not been on the internet today.

Birthdays are the worst. Do you wish everyone a Happy Birthday? I have a select group of birthday emojis that I use. I stopped doing wine, champagne, and beer ones because it seemed hypocritical from someone who writes about not drinking. Then I worried that people with weight problems, diabetes, or gluten intolerance might be offended by the cake one and the shiny ones might be offensive to the environmentalists who have sworn off glitter. Do they even do birthdays? Do their religions permit it? I think you get the point.

I spent my birthday at a conference a few years ago, and at lunchtime I checked Facebook. No one had wished me Happy Birthday. I wondered if it *was* my birthday. Maybe I was mistaken. Later in the day, I checked again, and still nothing. I finally discovered that I had made some changes to my privacy settings. If Facebook does not say it's your birthday, apparently it really isn't.

Posting on social media and not getting likes can feel like throwing a party where no one shows up. Everyone goes to everyone else's parties, so why don't they like yours? What do the people in the know do? Some of them pay for likes, which is akin to paying someone to come to your party. If you're in business, your social media presence is important, perhaps vital to your success, so it's understandable that getting likes or some reaction is important. Yet for most people it still feels like a rejection if our carefully crafted meme or photograph or witty comment does not get lots of positive reactions. When did this become so important? When did we all start needing admiration, adoration, and the confirmation that we are OK, that we are liked or even loved?

If you don't spend a lot of time on social media, you might wonder why this matters at all. It is part of a wider problem of our self-esteem being lowered by what other people are saying about us or even what they're not saying. The danger of overthinking is that it can paralyze us and stop us from doing anything, stifling our creativity and blocking us off from experimentation. Most things that people create are not good in the beginning. Virtually everything has to grow and develop into a more fully realized and finished product. Instead of obsessing on what everyone else thinks of your social media posts, try taking small risks or simply pushing good vibes out into the world. One helpful exercise in strengthening our emotional resilience and fighting imposter syndrome is to put something out there that you like, are happy with, and believe in, and then walk away without worrying how it's received. Don't look back. Don't check your likes every hour. Just let it be.

Stay in Your Own Lane

Does it seem that everyone around you is doing more with their time? We all have the same number of hours in the day and yet some people seem to spend theirs more productively. We don't really know how people spend their time. We know what they tell us and show us on social media, but just because someone is seemingly always busy does not mean that they are doing something useful with the time. Before you compare yourself to others, stop and remember that your time is best used on your projects. Figuring out how others are spending their time will not move you farther along, so don't get sucked into that game. Comparing our productivity with others is another form of self-sabotage, because while we are looking into their backyards, we are not getting our own work done.

Another way that you may be self-sabotaging yourself is by getting tied up with political stuff. Getting angry and frustrated about things posted online is a waste of your time and will ultimately add to your feeling of not being good enough. How are these things connected? If you are using your energy on another person's agenda, you are allowing yourself to believe that what they are saying should have your attention rather than your work, which is ultimately most important. If you see something that bothers you, ask yourself what you can do about it. Make a donation, write a letter, or call a congressional representative. Find a positive way to be supportive but step away from the negativity. Allowing yourself to become angry will not help your self-esteem.

Feeling like an imposter can mean that we are too afraid to

press the start button on our projects. Since I have helped people with publishing their books, I have learned of many people who have potential masterpieces sitting in desk drawers or on computers waiting to be completed. The only way we can ever become confident in our abilities to do anything is to do it.

Every single wonderful thing in life began somewhere:

A note becomes a symphony.

A word becomes a literary treasure.

A stitch becomes a tapestry.

A line of code becomes a best-selling app.

A pinch of salt becomes a gourmet meal.

A kind word becomes a friendship.

A brushstroke becomes a masterpiece.

Imagine if the person who discovered how to make chocolate gave up because the first attempt tasted too bitter. No invention or creation ever started out perfect. Whatever you are waiting to do, even if you waited a hundred years, it is unlikely that it would ever be exactly how you wanted it to be. Accepting that things are a little less polished than you would like will help you be more productive. Once you get started, you will get better. If you ever worry about imperfection, look at the reviews of your favorite book. There will always be one-star reviews, also check out travel sites and find a destination that you have been to and love. You will see that there are some negative reviews on almost everything. During research, I discovered that even some of the wonders of the world were left wanting. The Great Wall of China is "just alright, not great" and the Taj Mahal was considered "disappointing." Whatever you do, you won't please everyone, you might not even completely please yourself. It is so much better to get started, you might even find negative feedback is helpful in knowing what to do better next time.

7

THE CHALLENGE OF BEING DIFFERENT

If you fall outside the norm in who you are or where you live, work, or play, it's likely that you have felt the burden of being different. Being different, existing on the fringe, or simply being part of a minority can be isolating and add to those not-good-enough feelings that plague so many of us. When you think about it, we are all bound to feel like this at some point. Everyone has challenges, everyone has limitations, and everyone has doubts. The next time you struggle, take a moment to clearly identify the source of what you're feeling. Chances are it could fall into one of these categories:

Mental Health

Mental health issues, including clinical depression, can lead to feelings of worthlessness. I am not a doctor, but I want to be clear—if you have persistent feelings of worthlessness that won't go away or are thinking of harming yourself, you must get help. Sometimes it's hard to untangle the complicated condition that is depression. It's hard to differentiate between low self-esteem and a more serious pattern of behavior. You might not need a self-help book. You might need the help of a medical doctor or licensed psychotherapist. If you have tried a few things and nothing has worked and suspect you might be depressed, don't hesitate to seek help from a professional.

Physical Health

When we feel we are not good enough, we don't always take care of our health as well as we should. If you don't have the confidence to ask the correct questions from your health professional, you might not get the right care. It can be daunting and intimidating to ask probing and tough questions. I am not anti-medical, and I have generally had excellent treatment from my healthcare providers, yet I know that doctors and medical staff have limited time. We need to be honest and sometimes courageous with them, just as we need them to be open to seeing us as a whole person and treat us holistically.

We know ourselves more than someone who has just met us, and daring to speak up can be scary. When we are fortunate in dealing with professionals who take their time and listen to us, we have a better chance of having good results. If you ask a question of a medical professional and don't feel heard or understood, you might damage your health if you accept an unsatisfactory diagnosis. Information is power when it comes to your body and your well-being. You will need to learn to get comfortable asking awkward questions, and that starts with believing that you are worthy of having all the information you need.

There was a time when patients were discouraged, and in some places, not allowed to see their own medical charts when in hospital. Viewing the medic as an expert who has god-like status and stands above the patient in authority, makes it difficult for patients to question them.

Your health is also more likely to be a priority if you have self-respect and believe that you are worthy. Eating nutritious food, allowing yourself enough sleep and taking time to exercise can come at a cost of time, money or a sacrifice. Treat your body with disrespect, and you will suffer in the way you look and feel.

Menopause and Hormonal Issues

If you are a man, and you think this doesn't apply to you, think again. If you have women in your life and you care about them, which I'm sure you do, this information will be useful.

When you read or hear about menopause, you will rarely see mental health, confidence, or self-esteem discussed as part of the issue. While everyone is talking about hot flashes and weight gain—which are bad enough in themselves—the deeper and often more painful symptoms are those that affect women mentally. Again, I am not speaking as a medical professional but from personal experience and from conversations with many other women.

Hormones are evil. Some mornings over the past few years I have woken with a feeling of absolute hopelessness and dread. I couldn't think of anything I was good at, all my achievements seemed to mean nothing, and I did not understand what direction I needed to take. The next day I might feel excited and happy about life. Then later I felt angry, stressed, frustrated, sad, or hopeless. These changes in mood came out of nowhere. I can honestly say before I began the menopause journey, I experienced none of this. The worst part is that these feelings can compound feelings of imposter syndrome. I am speaking from personal experience and your mileage may vary, yet if you have found that you have feelings different from anything you have ever experienced, they could be linked to menopause. I must remind myself when I wake in the morning and feel hopeless that it may well be hormonal—especially when it changes so quickly in the span of a few hours.

Be supportive of the women in your life who might be experiencing menopause. Know that they might go through some scary and miserable symptoms. The physical stuff is bad enough—particularly lack of sleep, which makes everything worse—but they might also experience emotional and mental health issues that can be devastating. Menopause can be a life-changing event, and it can last for more than a decade. We should not dismiss it as psychosomatic, frivolous, or a minor discomfort that will be over in a matter of days.

I found that practicing self-care and compassion, along with eating better and exercising, helped tremendously. I also had to accept that wrinkles and loss of muscle mass that seemed to come overnight was a new normal. In my head, I'm still thirty, but then I look in the mirror. At that point, I try to remind myself that there will be an end to it. There will come a time when I won't have to deal with this kind of hormonal issue again. I can't wait!

Mid-Life Crisis

Menopause is a massive psychological as well as physical shift. As women's bodies change, so does their perceived usefulness. Society often judges women based on their looks. Perhaps you don't believe this is true, yet I can point you to news item that mention what a woman is wearing before anything about what she does or her achievements. We have a long way to go before we can say that women are valued based on their skills and not as a mannequin. Older women often talk about feeling invisible. If we are no longer sexually attractive, then what are we?

When we reach an age where we can no longer bear children, where any children we have are independent and possibly careers are shifting as we move towards retirement, it can be a time of reflection and wondering what it is all for. Have we achieved what we wanted to? Did our life go in the direction we hoped? Added to this, people around us start to die more frequently or develop physical illnesses, it can seem like we are at the beginning of the end.

You Are Not Alone

There are many ways that being different can make us feel like an Imposter. If you are struggling in any area of life, it is likely that someone else is too. Be encouraged by finding those who may experience something similar. Seek support groups. There are so many opportunities, especially online, where you can meet people who understand what you are dealing with. You can often be anonymous if you find it preferable.

8

YOU ARE GOOD ENOUGH TO GET THAT JOB!

I spent almost two decades helping people find and keep jobs. Confidence in job interviews is vital, and it is a lot simpler than people think.

Interviewers *want* to hire you. The job application process is costly and time-consuming, and employers don't want to take time out of their schedule to waste their time or yours. If you have reached the interview stage, you are already further along than most others. This is your time to shine. During my time helping prepare candidates for an interview, it shocked me to learn that those with everything the employer needed were sometimes unwilling to put in the work to make sure they had a successful interview. They seemed to think the interviewers should be able to read their mind.

When you attend an interview, you are conducting a sales negotiation. Your skills, your time and your expertise are for sale. When I taught interview skills, it surprised me to find that my students wanted to tell the interviewer all the negative things about them. I found it helpful to help them see themselves as salable. Though I hope by this point you have realized how amazing you are and that all the qualities you have that an employee really wants are within you, you will still have to do the work.

If you were selling a car, and you sold yourself like you previously have, you might not be showing yourself in the best light. "But I have to tell the truth," you say, because talented people lacking in confidence don't like to brag. Back to the car. Would you buy this one?

2012 Blue Model C Hooptie

- 100,000 miles on the clock
- Might not start on cold mornings
- Cigarette burns on back seat
- Window occasionally sticks
- Slower than most
- Smallish trunk

You would never advertise a car that way, right? Yet those who lack confidence constantly tell the interviewer information that is neither being asked for or required. You are there to sell your best features. A good interviewer will discover what they need without you volunteering stuff that they never asked for. Let's look at that car again. How could we describe it more favorably?

2012 Blue Model C Hooptie

- Reliable car with below average mileage
- Solid workhorse that has served one family for years
- Professionally maintained according to recommended schedule

- Deceptively spacious interior, clean, and well maintained with everything in working order
- Compact and perfect for parking in tight spots.

What Do Interviewers Want?

When I worked with new clients who had little experience being interviewed, many had a fixed idea about the person who they would be facing. Their lack of confidence often meant that they believed it was the interviewer's job to catch them out. As someone who had been on both sides of the recruitment desk, I know the opposite is true. The process is time-consuming and costly, and the company doing the hiring wants nothing more than to get the right person for the job on the first attempt. Advertising, arranging the interviews and key team members taking time out of their workday means it benefits everyone involved to get the right person.

A hiring manager interviewed about what she looked for in a new hire highlighted these three qualities as key:

- Ability to do the job
- Ability to fit in with the team
- Loyalty and reliability

Attitude is often more important than the job skills. We can learn skills along the way, showing up and being a team player isn't as easy to teach.

Now that you know the employer would like to hire you, it's time to prepare yourself. Remember that car we were selling? Now is the time to spruce it up and show its best features. A person sitting behind a desk cannot read your mind. Many of the job seekers I met would have the notion that a stranger would already know information about them. The stuff that appears obvious to you and therefore not considered important may well be the factor that could land you the job. When I sat on an interview panel and knew the person sat before me. I couldn't, in the interests of fairness, bring up information not disclosed on their application or that they hadn't volunteered. It was frustrating to know that they were omitting the very skills or experience that would put them above the other candidates.

To make sure you do not make this mistake, go through your application and practice questions with someone you trust and knows your history. They can help you fill in the gaps and prompt you with forgotten skills. Putting together an inventory of your skills and abilities is the perfect way to build your confidence. Remember, you are not comparing yourself with others; you are proving you have what the role requires.

Don't Skip the Prep

It is rare that a person can walk into an interview without preparation and be successful. Getting a job can be like a job in itself, there is work involved. I will break down some steps for you so the next time you have a job interview you will have a much better chance of succeeding. This is presuming that you have already completed the application or submitted the résumé. The application part of the process is to help you get the interview. Once you have an interview, you can show the best version of you. Many people skip this part in the belief that because they have the skills required that the employer should know this instinctively and should just offer them the job. You don't know who you are competing against, and it would be remiss of you to not take full advantage of the preparation part and inventory of your skills and abilities.

Before the Interview

Research is a key skill that will put you ahead of the game. What do you know about the company you're applying to work with?

There is no excuse today for not doing a full investigation into the company. When you arrive, be prepared to demonstrate that you have done your homework, so that it's clear you are invested in its mission and that the job in question is a role that you really want.

Chances are, they are not looking for a superstar who might use the role as a stepping-stone. They want someone who will become a vital part of the team. The stakes are high for everyone involved in an interview, yet as applicants we often believe that we are in the weaker position. In fact, we have something that the employer really needs. The interview is showing them we have the skills they need and that we are the right person for the job, so why would you not do as much preparation as possible? When I taught interview preparation skills in the early 1990s, the internet was very new, and people were not really using it for preparation; they had to go to much greater lengths to discover information about the company they were applying to. Now you can find virtually everything you need to know at the touch of a few keystrokes, however, there are other things you can do to make sure you are in the lead in the interview game.

Besides researching general information about the company, learning what innovative things they've been doing: who they've hired, what contracts they have, their values, can all help to show that you really are interested in this job. Everyone likes to be flattered when it is genuine and taking an interest in the company is very flattering.

When waiting for your interview, I encourage you to look around the waiting area. What can you learn from the information on noticeboards? Is there a company magazine or brochure? You might get a good idea of the company's values just by how they decorate the waiting area. Does it appear that they embrace new thinking or new technologies or are they more traditional? Paying attention can help you frame your interview answers and questions more appropriately.

Do you know anyone who already works for the company or organization? What can they tell you that you might not discover via traditional routes that would be helpful for you to know? Be your own private detective, because doing your homework will pay dividends later.

What you wear to a job interview can be influenced by what you can discover about the company. It's helpful to know what kind of culture they embrace. Be sure to dress appropriately. You can rarely be overdressed but easily underdressed. Even if the company takes a relaxed approach to workplace attire, be careful not to be too casual. It's a business meeting, and, no, they don't have to accept you as you are. Whatever happens after you accept the position differs from what happens when you are still at the negotiation stage. The interview is where you need to be on your best behavior. For example, if you have a nose ring, unless you are sure that the company is an ardent supporter or manufacturer of nose rings, you would be wise to take it out. And though tattoos are popular nowadays, it might be worth figuring out if the company has a policy on covering them until you get the job.

The person sitting behind the desk often makes a judgment about you within the first minute, and if they have an unconscious bias, you will have to work harder to gain their approval and interest. It is better not to put barriers between you and the interviewer

Checklist: Before the Interview

- Remember, they want to hire someone. Why not you?
- Do your research.
- Prepare your interview wardrobe. Is it ready to wear? Do you have accessories?
- Have at least three key selling points showing that you are perfect for the role.

- Prepare answers to obvious questions.
- Practice answers to difficult questions.
- Write questions you want to ask.
- Check your social media feed—make sure it's all positive.
- Plan how you will get to the interview.

At the Interview

Your interviewer may not be trained or skilled. They might have been promoted into the role or have to step in at the last minute. Bear this in mind as you go through the interview process. The interviewer might be more nervous than you are, so help them out if they seem to struggle to ask the right questions. If they are not good at asking follow-up questions, have answers in place and make sure they do not have to work to get the information from you. This is where practice and preparation become your superpower.

Questions

Other than curveball questions, it is usually easy to figure out what an employer will ask you in an interview. Think about it— if you were interviewing a potential employee, what would you want to know? Study the job description, learn all you can about the company, and then think about what they need to know to make sure you are the best person for the job. Pre-empt the questions that they might ask and write them down. You can also co-opt a friend to help you out with this by letting them interview you and give you honest feedback. Or you could ask a local company to give you a mock interview before you even begin the application process. Many welcome the opportunity to give their managers experience.

Interview questions are not a mystery, especially if you have a good interviewer. There are some solid and predictable questions, and you need to make sure you have answers ahead of time. You also need to have concise and plausible answers to any problematic questions. It's not smart to wing it on that one question you are dreading, the one you know will make you struggle and feel awkward. Have an honest discussion with yourself and think about how you can best answer that question and still be seen in a good light. Make sure that you can look the interviewer in the eye, so they trust what you are saying.

I worked with clients who had criminal records and needed to show that they were rehabilitated. They were often excellent candidates who could do the job, so this needed delicate preparation to assure the interviewer that they would be a good fit. They had to practice telling the story of making a mistake, regretting it, and paying their dues. They had to present themselves as a fully participating member of society. Preparing well showed the hiring manager they were not afraid of this question coming up. Different countries, states, and territories might have different rules regarding what an employer can ask you, but in the day of social media, they can find out pretty much whatever they want.

Be prepared to have some questions of your own. What do you want to know about the company? I'm not talking about salary or benefits. Think of what would impress you if someone asked the question. For example, you might have discovered that they have a new contract overseas, and you could ask if that means that the position has a requirement for travel, showing that you are really interested in or would be available for that aspect of the job.

Social Media

Although you may believe that your social media profile is private, that you have all the precautions in place so it's not shared or seen by anyone except for your close family and friends, anyone can take a screenshot of your information. Or maybe you posted something a long time ago and you've forgotten about it. It might come back to haunt you in the future. Everything on social media is somewhere forever, and some of your previous posts might not show you in the best light.

The information, memes, and opinions that you share tell a story of you and your values. A seemingly innocent meme taken out of context can end a career, so don't let it be yours.

Something else that could show up on social media are naked photos. "It's only between us," they said when that person asked you to pose for the video or photographs that, looking back, you realize would not look out of place on a porn site. And maybe that is where they ended up. If you struggle with confidence or self-esteem, it might seem flattering that someone wants to take and keep naked images or videos of you. Once your personal image is captured, however, it is out of your control. Even if it is on your device, it can be hacked. For celebrities, a sex tape might boost their careers. For the rest of us, it will only bring embarrassment and the possibility of losing a position or damaging our business. And then there is the possibility of it being used as revenge porn when a relationship ends acrimoniously. It is your choice though worth thinking carefully about. An artistically shot boudoir photo session might make you feel confident and gorgeous but waking up to see your nether regions displayed wide open on everyone's Twitter feed is unlikely to have the same effect. It is hard to know how you will feel about something in a few years' time. Whatever your decision, make sure it is yours, and do not be pressured to be part of something that makes you uncomfortable. If your gut instinct tells you it's a bad idea—listen.

Checklist: At the Interview

- Breathe.
- Take opportunity to learn more about the company.
- Handshake.
- Eye contact.
- Smile.
- Help the interviewer out.
- Be your best self.

Remote Interviews

For interviews conducted remotely, much of the above may not apply. Plan for success in online interviews too.

- Make sure that your workstation is clear, and you have everything you need.
- Check what is visible behind you.
- What will the interviewer be able to see, is it professional and appropriate?
- Dress for success. Remember, they can see you, so even if you are at home, your pajamas are not suitable attire.
- Minimize distractions, these could include children, pets, visitors to your home, garbage pickup, mail deliveries etc.
- Look at your calendar and plan so you will give yourself the best chance to have a quiet and uninterrupted meeting.

After the Interview -Dealing with Rejection

A job application rejection can knock your confidence, yet it can be a valuable piece of data that you can use for future interviews. You can ask for feedback from your interviewer. If you don't ask, you will never know and therefore not be able to make adjustments. They might say no, or you might find some who will not only give you feedback on your performance but will also offer suggestions on how you could be better prepared. When good jobs are in short supply, there will always be an abundance of good candidates. You might not be the best person for the job in every situation. This does not mean that you shouldn't stay focused on your success even after they have concluded the interview process. The first person offered the job does not always accept the position. A candidate might have multiple interviews and take a different offer. This puts the interviewer in the position of having to either offer the position to another candidate or start the process all over again, costing more time and resources. To be sure they keep you in mind, there are steps you can take:

Send a Thank You Note

When a thoughtful, handwritten note lands on the desk of a hard-working recruitment manager, it is likely to make their day. It might also encourage them to go look at your application again to see if you might be suitable for another position.

Be Memorable—For the Right Reasons

Let's go back to your interview for a moment. Imagine that we rewind the tape and you're watching yourself in fast-forward going through the interview process. You arrived, you read the company magazines, you researched, you looked on the noticeboard to see if there was anything you could discover; you talked politely to the receptionist. If appropriate, did you greet the person warmly and in a friendly manner? Did you shake hands? Did you smile? Did you use positive body language?

Did you sit and look confident? Did you fidget? When the janitorial staff came around, did you move your feet so they could get around? Were you respectful and friendly? Did you hold the door open for the person behind you? Did you help that person with the bags? Did you appear helpful or self-absorbed? When you attend an interview, you are presenting your whole self for inspection, so make sure you behave respectfully and appropriately from the moment you arrive and throughout the entire process.

When I worked for an organization that hired employees, I didn't sit on the interview panel. My job was to offer a tour of the workplace, and this part of the process was vital. How the applicant treated me and behaved in my presence when their guard was down, often showed more than they disclosed in the interview. They didn't know who I was or if I had any influence, but I did, and I could report my findings to the hiring panel.

Checklist: After the Interview

- Follow up.
- Ask for feedback.
- Make notes.
- Send a thank-you card.

9

CREATING A CONFIDENT YOU

It all starts with you. Wherever you came from doesn't matter—OK, it matters to the extent that some have a better start in life than others, yet we know that where you start doesn't have to dictate where you end up. You can always *restart*. Now is the best time in history to do something new. There are mountains of free resources, educational opportunities, and people who want to help. You are good enough. Yes, you might need to get better at some things, and that is where your confidence will come from.

At first it might seem hard to deconstruct much of your thinking and your belief system, but if it hasn't been working for you, there is no benefit to hanging on to it. It starts with getting to know yourself, what you like, what you want to do with your time. Self-confidence grows as you learn to do the things you want to do, though at first it is hard to know what that is. What in your life makes you feel good? What are the things you claim to enjoy but really do only to please others? If you could, what kinds of activities would you do instead?

Example: You might go to a football game because it is what

your spouse or friends like, and you enjoy being part of the crowd. You might have previously enjoyed it, and now it is part of your routine. Or you might do it and try to convince yourself that you like it when secretly or even unconsciously without you knowing it, you don't enjoy it and might resent it. When you finally come around to deciding to say no to taking part in an activity that you don't enjoy, you will feel empowered. As you build this confidence muscle, it will become stronger and easier to use. What more powerful indicator is there that you are good enough that you make your own choices? Look at those you admire or even envy. Do they spend their precious time doing things they don't want to do? And I don't mean doing things selflessly for other people, I mean consistently making choices against their own interests and preferences. Let's look at some examples:

Job

Do you like your work? Do you feel satisfaction, joy, and fulfillment? Or do you feel miserable, like time is passing you by? Do you feel you could do something better? Do you feel you are not making a difference and not using your talents?

Romantic Relationships

Do you feel fulfilled, valued, loved, treasured, heard? Do you feel good imagining spending the rest of your life with your current significant other? Do you feel unappreciated, belittled, tolerated, despised? Are you often unhappy?

Friendships

Do your friendships bring you joy and make you smile? Are your friends there for you when you need them? Do you feel you do all the running, all the work? Can you be yourself when you are with your friends? Do you feel you have to pretend to fit in to be loved?

Hobbies and Interests

When you think about the activities you do in your free time, do you feel excited, energized, and happy? Or do you do them because you always have, and it's expected of you? For instance, if you were on vacation with a group of friends and a certain activity was planned, but no one would know if you had participated or not, would you still go? If you ditched it, would you miss it? Does it put a frown on your face, or does it make you smile? These answers are important because what we do with our time signals how much value we place on our own happiness.

Will I Become Selfish?

Yes, and about time too. Being selfish in some areas of your life is not a bad thing. If you were completely unselfish, you would eat the bare minimum required to survive and give everything you own to those in need. A self-centered person who does everything for themselves and does not care about others would not be reading this book. I want to shift the pendulum, so you feel a little more selfish, more deserving, and good enough, because being good enough is being worthy of value.

Where Else Are You Giving up Power?

Your kids? Everyone has to sacrifice for their kids and do their best for them, yet do you have to do everything for them? Do you have to give up on your dreams so they can live theirs? If you love ferrying your kids to every after-school activity and standing on the sidelines cheering them on, I salute you, yet as they get older and can get to places by themselves, do you have to? I don't have biological kids. I am, however, a stepparent. I learned quickly that there are things you should do for your kids and others that are their business. My stepson played football. I have zero interest but was keen to do all the things his mom entrusted me with when he came to live with his father and me. I went to booster club meetings and felt like a fish out of water. My husband said he had no intention of being involved in that side of things. After a few meetings, I realized I could still be supportive without doing things exactly the way his mom did. I still picked him up and dropped him off to meetings, but decided the fundraising was not my responsibility. This was his hobby. As a Brit, I find the obsession with sports strange, and there seemed a much stronger expectation for me to support the sports activities than the academic side. Trust me, I took that part seriously!

Are you judging me? I am OK with that because I have spent so much time judging myself that I have worked on developing the muscle that says, "Nope, not doing that!" I'm not a hardass by any means, but there are some things we have to learn to be firm about. We still expect women to take up the lion's share of the work more readily than men. When my son said he didn't enjoy taking the school bus and wanted me to drive him to school and pick him up, it was a firm no. His dad would not have considered it, and wouldn't be asked, and we were both in full-time jobs.

Are you ready to get started flexing those confidence muscles and get rid of your imposter syndrome? Let's get started.

PART II

YOUR 28-DAY PLAN

You can either use a notebook or the notes boxes at the end of each section and plot your confident future.

Jump in and do the whole thing in one month or take it gently at whatever pace works for you. Just do it soon! Even if you start with one challenge per week.

How Will Doing This Make Me Feel That I'm Good Enough?

If you can't even find the time to do what you want, to live your life on your terms, what is that saying to you? If you are not worth the effort of finding out what you like and dislike, if you have spent so much time living your life to please other people, it will take some time for you to get used to pleasing yourself.

Before you take action, read through each section and pinpoint the days where you will need to plan in advance. Make a note of days where you cannot do certain activities, move them around and plan accordingly. You will get the most benefit if you do as many as possible close together. Remember this is about showing you that you are good enough and you deserve to take care of yourself, skipping the nurturing or challenging parts signals to yourself that you are not worthy.

This is NOT a Challenge!

This is not about making you do stuff you don't want to do, part of doing it might at first make you feel uncomfortable, yet ultimately the doing will make you feel better.

Do I Have to Do Them All?

Some may need time or resources you don't yet have. Aim to do as many as possible and check them off as you do them. Read through the list and decide in advance what you know you can do and set yourself a deadline.

Day One Preparation—Remember

Find a quiet spot. Think about the first memory when you were really happy. What were you doing? Who were you with? What were you seeing? Hearing? Feeling? Thinking?

If your memories come in random timelines, that's OK just think about times when you were really happy. It is vital that you only list things that make YOU happy not that you remember other people telling you they enjoyed when they were with you. What did YOU enjoy? What DO you enjoy?

Prompts: Think about Your Best:
Vacation
Night out
Creative activity
Job/volunteer opportunity

Hobby
Time spent alone
Book
Physical activity
Conversations
People
Meal
Restaurant
Time with animals
Time with children
Theatrical experience

What makes you come alive? Of these, what jumps out that you would like to do again?

Day Two: Preparation—Dream

Imagine you wake up tomorrow and can do whatever you want and have all the resources you need.

Write everything that you can think of that you would like to do.

Day Three: Preparation – Let go

What Would You: Stop Doing?

Leave out?
Who would you spend less time with?
Where would you stop going?
What would you stop eating, drinking, reading, watching?

Day Four: Preparation—Recognize Your Achievements

You are good at so many things; you need to remind yourself of them. List your achievements large or small. Anything and everything that you are remotely proud of or that someone else says you are good at. This will be an ongoing list that you will add to regularly. If you struggle to come up with ideas, ask someone you trust to write three positive things about you. I know this may be difficult or awkward, yet people are usually only too happy to help.

You could ask.
What do I do that you value?
What positive trait would you mention if you were telling someone about me?

Prompts

Educational and job achievements.
Fund raising / Event planning.
Hobbies / Athletic achievements.

Day Five: Go

Somewhere on your own. It doesn't have to be something big, just something that you would normally do with other people that can be equally enjoyable doing alone.

Idea: The Movies

It's fun to do things with others but have you noticed that when a group is trying to choose a movie, once you have discounted the ones that someone in the group is opposed to seeing, you are left with a lukewarm choice that no one is against, yet no one feels passionate about either. Find a movie you want to go see, that no one else does, whether it's a kid's movie you always liked or a French Art House movie, whatever it is, go. Put it out there that you are going and be open to someone coming with you, but only if they want to see your choice. Don't let anyone ruin your fun, if in doubt go alone. Or go to a Symphony, Ballet. Comedy show, art gallery, a baseball game, meditation class, widget store. Anywhere that YOU want to go.

Where did you go?
How did you feel?

Day Six: Ask

When we struggle with imposter syndrome, we may not be comfortable asking for things for ourselves. Not only are you believing that you are less than worthy by not daring to ask, you are also not giving others the opportunity to help you. Giving is a gift that many people enjoy, and we can get more pleasure from it than receiving. What could you ask someone to do for you they may not know that you need or want?

Suggestions

Have someone feed your dog, cat or tarantula.
Write a review or testimonial.
Share a post.
Water your plants.
Give their honest opinion.
Go somewhere with you.
Sign a petition.
Volunteer at an event.

The trick with asking is not to be offended if they say no. We have no right to have expectations of others when we are asking for favors. We may ask, and they may say no. You might find it easier to ask people you don't know. Asking for donations or support in some area can be a good way to stretch ourselves. Just start somewhere and grow your confidence.

CASE STUDY

One of my least favorite activities is going to have work done on my car, even an oil change. There's usually a lot of hanging around and I have to sit somewhere where there's often a TV on that is showing a program I don't want to watch, or cable news of the worst kind. I don't want to waste my time on it however I have not found a suitable way around it until recently.

My husband suggested I ask them to drive me home, as where he goes, they provide a shuttle. On my most recent visit for an oil change, I asked if there was a shuttle; they told me there wasn't. I then was a little bolder I asked if they had somewhere that I could work as I didn't want to sit in the room with the TV on. They offered me the use of an office. Score, I've never thought about this before, but there are plenty of quiet places in the showroom and they were happy to let me use one for an hour. I got some work done, and I had grown my confidence by asking for something I wanted. I also discovered chatting with someone as I left that there is no set TV channel and it's perfectly OK to turn it over or even turn it off. These are tiny victories; however they build up a set of strategies and confidences, that we can use, adapt and learn from and add to our future growth.

What did you ask for?
How did you feel?

Day Seven: Wear

Wear a favorite outfit. Even if you are not going anywhere, wear it to the shops, make yourself feel and look amazing. Enjoy the sensation of being dressed for success all day. You might find that you want to do something to match your outfit. Or wear something that you have not before that makes you feel good but maybe that other people disapprove of. The fashion police have no power over you. I encourage you to WEAR WHAT YOU WANT Whatever your age.

What did you wear?
How did it make you feel?

Day Eight: Eat

You know that place that you pass on the side of the road? The cafe where you've always wondered what it's like inside but never dared go in? Or the food trucks you have never been to because you are not sure what food they serve? Make plans to go to one of those places.

Or Dine Upmarket

Dress up and eat at a restaurant alone. Be as adventurous as you dare. Don't hide behind a book or your phone. Order something delicious and savor it. Dare to try something different. Or as I saw someone doing recently, ask the server to bring you something that will surprise you, you can always give them parameters although the less the better to allow for a daring surprise.

What did you eat?
How did you feel?

Day Nine: Say

Affirmations are powerful, there is a good reason successful people say them regularly. Find some that resonate with you and create a habit of doing them daily. Here's a list of suggestions, adjust them to what feels right for you. Choose or create three and say them when you get up in the morning or whenever you take a break, choose one that you can do from memory when you are driving and say them before you go to sleep. You might find it useful to have a sticky note with your affirmation on your bathroom mirror or in your closet. Just make sure to put them in a prominent place where you are likely to see them.

Suggestions

My past does not define me.
I can do anything I want.
This is my life, and I live it how I choose.
I am ready to begin my new life today.
I am skilled and efficient.
I am daring and creative.
My life is full of possibilities.
I am every bit as good as everyone else.
I have big dreams, and I will achieve them.
I put myself first.
I deserve happiness.
The best is yet to come.
Every day I become more confident.
I am happy, and I am well.
I deserve the best.
I am attracting good things.
I love my life.

Add Some Gratitude

Those who express gratitude find more to be grateful for. Look around you and think about all that you have that you would miss if it wasn't there.

Write your favorite affirmations.

Day Ten: See

Imagining how you want your life to be is visualizing. Visualizations work best when you can see, feel or imagine the outcome you want. You may not believe it in the beginning, having a strong desire will help. Whatever you visualize, you will need to take action. Our mind wants to know what our destination is. If we don't know where we want to go, we have no way of getting there. Success does not happen by accident. When we don't believe in ourselves it is hard at first to imagine being successful, this will need practice and therefore I will take you step by step. The clearer you are in what you want the better your outcome will be. Everyone visualizes differently. There are no wrong ways to do it, as long as you focus on positive outcomes. Some people struggle to see things in their mind's eye and if that is you, try doing it by imagining feelings or sounds.

Think big. At first you may feel silly imagining yourself being wildly successful, please trust me when I tell you that is how successful people do it. They see themselves clearly where they want to be and keep seeing it in their mind's eye until it becomes their reality. Begin by thinking about what you want, start by choosing an area of your life.

Visualization Process

Think about what you want, you can create both short- and long-term goals, begin with something simple. Suggested areas are health, wellness, finance, or relationships.

- Get a picture in your mind of how that will look.
- Make the picture as real as possible.
- If you find it difficult to visualize, imagine you are

creating a story or a movie with you as the main character.

- Imagine what you will see, hear, feel, smell, taste.
- Add as many details as possible—people, furniture, landscape, movement, words, music.
- Add what you are wearing and recognize how you feel in your clothes.
- Keep adding details until it is bigger, brighter, and more powerful.
- Make sure you are in the picture as if you are looking through your own eyes.
- Imagine stepping out of the picture, see what you look like as if you are looking at yourself.
- Step back into the picture again as if you are looking through your own eyes.
- Continue to build the feeling and add even more details.
- When you have created a picture that really feels like one you can believe in and see yourself enjoying, practice for a few minutes every day with no other distractions. Find a quiet spot and close your eyes and see yourself living the future that you want.

Describe your visualization

Day Eleven: Buy

Treat yourself to something. It doesn't have to be costly. Just a treat for you.

Inexpensive

A fruit you have never tasted.
A candy bar you enjoyed as a child.
A motivational poster.
A new toothbrush.
A picture frame that you can put your favorite photograph or print out your affirmations or a certificate of achievement.
A magazine with beautiful photographs of clothes you will soon be wearing.

Mid-Range

A journal. If you don't want to use the note sections of this book, you could get a journal to document your journey or simply to write your thoughts, hopes and your dreams.
You can write in it now or you can decide what you want its purpose to be, you might also want to buy a beautiful pen to go with it.
A travel book to places where you want to go.
A houseplant.
Something that smells nice-an essential oil or perfume.
New underwear.
A hardcover book that's brand new that you are the first to read.

Pricier

New exercise gear or running shoes.
Good quality bedding.
A fruit tree you can plant and nurture.
A new outfit.
A gadget that will support your goal.
The item is not important the value that you place on yourself in
allowing yourself to have it, is.

What did you buy?
How did you feel?

Day Twelve: Help

Offer to help someone in need. Give a gift of your time to someone who you know will appreciate it. It doesn't have to be someone you know. You could help at a homeless shelter or animal sanctuary. Giving a little to someone else can lift us up. Help can also be something as simple as reaching out to a friend, checking in on a neighbor or doing any act of kindness. Sometimes we forget to be kind when we are wrapped up in ourselves. If you don't feel that you are good enough then giving to others might not be top of your list of things to do. I can almost guarantee you will feel better. Looking outside of ourselves is a good antidote to overthinking.

Who did you help?
How did you feel?

Day Thirteen: Stop

It's time to say no to something you have been doing for a long time that no longer serves you or makes you happy. Write the resignation letter, quit the gym you no longer attend. End the expensive membership. Or maybe it's a hobby you have been doing that really has been for someone else and not for you. Do not use this as an excuse to quit something you want to do but are scared to.

What did you quit?
How did you feel?

Day Fourteen: Read

Read something you've always wanted to that you worry you might be judged on, a children's book, a trashy novel, a sci-fi book. Allow yourself to do something just because you want to. You can also use this space to write a list of all the books that you want to read. Come back and check off the list whenever you have found time to read them.

What did you read?
How did you feel?

Day Fifteen: Rebel

Stand up for yourself, in love and kindness, say what you are unhappy about. Those of us who have spent a lifetime worrying about what people think of us can find it hard to speak up. You are worthy of respect and need not be patronized or negatively treated. If you have always been the person to let it go, it can be quite a shock to those in your life to discover the new you. They will get over it. If you are unsure if it is them, or if you might be overly sensitive, try to imagine them saying the same thing to someone else. Think of a person who the offender holds in high esteem, would they ever speak to them the way they speak to you? This can also be important when someone disrespects your time. If someone is constantly showing you they do not value you or your time by showing up late or canceling on you, it is time to speak up. People will only treat you how you allow them to.

Who did you stand up to?
How did it go?

Day Sixteen: Detach

From someone or something that makes you unhappy. You don't have to be rude; you don't have to explain yourself, yet if someone in your life is causing you emotional pain it may be time to let them go. It is tough, especially when it is a family member or someone who has been in your life for a long time, yet we know when it is time. If you are constantly being undermined, or the relationship feels one-sided, then it could be time for a break or to disconnect completely.

Telephones, I often remind myself, work in both directions. If you are the person who is always chasing a relationship to keep it alive, then maybe a test would be to stop and see what happens. Some friendships are for a season and there comes a time when we need to let them go, or they might develop into a different type of relationship. Allow yourself to discover what life might be like if you were to let it go.

What did you disconnect from?
How did you feel?

Day Seventeen: Create

Make something. Unleash your creative side.

Suggestions.

Draw.
Paint a room.
Bake a cake.
Sew something, brighten up an item.
Handwrite a note.
Change your hairstyle or color.
Decorate a room.
Put up a shelf.
Rearrange your furniture.
Plant a tree.

What did you make?
How did you feel?

Day Eighteen: Change Your Mind

Change your mind about something, let someone down gently, say you can't go. Give yourself permission to say no.

What did you do?
How did you feel?

"Let the beauty of
what you love be
what you do."
Rumi

Day Nineteen: Watch

Something you like and no one else does on TV, or on a streaming service.

What did you watch? How did you feel?

Day Twenty: Detox

Detox from social media. If your work or other commitments makes this difficult, plan a few hours off. Make sure you don't allow yourself to make excuses. Do they really need you, will Facebook not survive without you for a day? Turn off all notifications and tell everyone who might need to know that you will be unavailable except for emergencies.

What did you detox from and for how long?
How did you feel?

Day Twenty-One: Shop

Go shopping and try on clothes that you normally wouldn't or haven't because someone else has discouraged you. Try it out, you might find that you don't like them, that doesn't matter. If you can afford it, pay someone to help you, a personal shopper, or a stylist, stores sometimes do this for free. Just get used to experimenting with yourself.

What did you try?
How did you feel?

Day Twenty-Two: Learn

Do something wonderful for yourself. This can be as simple or as lavish as time and resources allow. Local libraries and community centers have classes that are often low cost or free.

Ideas:

- Coding
- Aerial Yoga
- Art classes
- Ancestry classes
- Learn to play chess

You are smarter than you have believed and when you figure this out you will feel so much more confident about yourself. Just because you have never tried something does not mean that you will not be good at it. And remember that when you try something for the first time, you must get used to it. It might take you some time to learn something new or even to get started, don't allow this to discourage you.

What did you learn?
How did you feel?

Day Twenty-Three: Do

What have you always wondered about doing and put off because you worried what people might think? I did some pole fitness classes that were amazing exercise. I laughed to myself that if I was involved in an accident, it would leave my husband wondering what I was doing in the middle of the day, dressed in booty shorts without my wedding ring. (You take off your rings to avoid scratching the pole).

You may not want to do anything dramatic just something that you have always wanted to do. I have recently started to feed and observe birds in my yard. I fill the bird feeders daily and am learning to recognize the different birdsong, a few years ago this would have seemed dull. Now I love it, my choice, it is between me and the birds—no one else.

What did you do?
How did you feel?

Day Twenty-Four: Fix

Look around and find something that needs repairing or updating. A watch needing a battery, a leaky faucet, a lightbulb long dead, boots that need shining. You deserve to be surrounded by things that work. As I was writing this, we were putting out Christmas decorations, the reindeer that was previously placed outside only illuminated about a third of the way, and my husband was ready to trash it. As one of my goals is to toss fewer things and reduce the amount of stuff that will go into the landfill, I was determined to try to fix it. While removing every lightbulb in the failing section and testing each one, I was almost ready to admit defeat. Then I saw one gap where a lightbulb should be. I replaced it and was delighted when it worked. Yes, I could have spent the time better, or could I? The time spent was relaxing and meditative, the results were satisfying, and I didn't waste a resource.

What did you fix?
How did you feel?

Day Twenty-Five: Delegate

Something you don't enjoy doing or know someone else could do better? Best scenario: If you can afford to, pay someone to do it. Hiring someone and having the courage to tell them what you want and how you want it done is empowering. It could be hiring a cleaner for a few hours or a virtual assistant online. If you have never paid anyone to do anything, you will soon learn it is an excellent lesson in confidence building.

Asking for something to be done exactly the way you want may be hard at first, it is tempting to take the easy option and accept someone else's version of "good enough." Taking a deep breath and asking for what you really want is vital to your growth. If you are not able to pay, consider trading services.

What did you delegate?
How did you feel?

Day Twenty-Six: Travel and Experience

Have you ever gone anywhere alone or is there somewhere that you have always wanted to go but haven't because of people-pleasing behavior? For example: you don't go abroad because your partner doesn't enjoy flying or you've never been on a boat because they get seasick. How about doing it with someone else, alone or with a group? My husband always wants the aisle seat when we fly which means I always get the middle seat. I recently traveled alone and had the window seat and remembered how much I enjoyed looking out at the view on takeoff and landing. On my return I told him that next time we travel I planned to have the window seat; we don't have to sit together it's not like we talk much on planes. He was completely in agreement; you see he didn't force me to have the middle seat; he chose the aisle and people pleaser here did what I thought was right. I might even sit in a different row from him next time!

Always be mindful of your safety.

Where did you go?
How did you feel?

Day Twenty-Seven: Commit

What have you always wanted to do that you have been afraid of doing or not felt that you are good enough or capable of? Now that you have taken small steps to find what makes you happy and what doesn't and got a little out of your comfort zone, it's time to do something more daring.

- Sign up for a college class.
- Apply for a new job.
- Commit to a new exercise program.
- Sign up for a half marathon or start with a 5K or fun run.
- Go on a date.
- Look for a new home.

Anything new and daring that you've worried about for a long time and not felt capable of. What else do you need to do to feel more courageous and confident?

What did you do?
How did you feel?

Day Twenty-Eight: What else do you want to do?

Use the following pages to add anything you want to achieve, add to it whenever you think of something, check it off when you have done one and add a new item.

Short Term

Long term

Sometime

THE WORLD NEEDS YOU

I hope you have had many "aha" moments throughout this book. You read this for a reason and therefore I'm sure that some of it will have resonated with you.

During my preparation, I talked to a range of people and learned of their struggles. Imposter syndrome, lack of confidence, and overthinking covers a broad spectrum of people, and you could be at any point on it.

If you are struggling with overwhelming feelings, I encourage you to find a therapist or to talk to someone. Self-care is important, and it doesn't have to be confined to the odd massage. Ongoing and regular activities that will enhance your well-being are vital to your new life.

You are worth it.
You are here for a reason.
The world needs you.
It's not too late.
You can do it your way.
I believe in you.

Find your people.
Share your secrets.

If you need further help, I have a range of free videos on my YouTube channel YouTube.com/trishtaylorcoaching. They include techniques to let go of stress and help you build confidence.

Whatever you need, you are not alone. You are one of many who struggle with this issue, and yet by reading to the end of this book, you have made a firm commitment to make a change. I want to see you grow and thrive and be able to make a difference to the world. We are here because we have something that somebody needs. You are good enough, and you need to be reminded of it every now and again. If you don't do what you are here for, the world will miss it, and many will lose out on what you have to offer. Think of all the leaders who had an idea that became a vision and changed lives. They weren't all sure that it would work or that they were good enough.

As you grow and recognize your worth, you will find your place and your destiny. Your journey begins here and now. You deserve a wonderful, confident life. Now is the perfect time.

Trish

ABOUT THE AUTHOR

Trish Taylor was living and working in England, happily settled in her 14-year role as a career counselor and part-time jazz singer. An encounter with a Salsa-dancing American literally swept her off her feet. They married and moved to the United States. After working as a Mindset Coach and trainer, she has now moved into writing full-time. She is the author of a range of self-help books:

Why Am I Scared? Face Your Fears and Learn to Let Them Go.
I'm Never Drinking Again: Maybe It's Time to Think About Your Drinking?
Co-author of *Respect in the Workplace: You Have to Give it to Get it.*

Her latest book is a humorous travel guide:
Put the Kettle On: An American's Guide to British Slang, Telly and Tea.

Trish is currently working on her first fiction book.

Connect at www.trishtaylorauthor.com.

Printed in Great Britain
by Amazon

65613797R00083